English Reading Comprehension
For the Spanish Speaker

Book 3

For Ages 10 - Adult

Written by
Kathleen Fisher

Illustrated by
Richard Bao and **Paul Widosh**

Fisher Hill   Huntington Beach   California

Published by FISHER HILL
5267 Warner Avenue, #166
Huntington Beach, CA 92649-4079

Made in the U.S.A.

Publisher's Cataloging in Publication

Fisher, Kathleen S., 1952-
    English reading comprehension for the Spanish speaker.
Book 1 / by Kathleen Fisher. --1st ed.
    p. cm.
    Audience: Ages 10-adult.
    Includes bibliographical references and index.
    ISBN 13: 978-1-878253-44-6; ISBN 10: 1-878253-44-1

    1. English language--Textbooks for foreign speakers--
Spanish. 2. English as a second language.

Table of Contents

Contenido

Introduction

The purpose of this book is to help Spanish speakers improve their English reading comprehension skills. Reading comprehension is the ability to draw meaning from written words. This is an excellent book to use after finishing *English Reading Comprehension for The Spanish Speaker Book 2* and *English Reading and Spelling for the Spanish Speaker Book 3*.

This book is made up of twenty lessons. Lessons include practice with fluency, vocabulary, visualization, comprehension, and phonology or phonics. There is an answer key at the end of each lesson.

Reading smoothly (fluency) is an important skill. Fluency allows readers to think about what they are reading instead of having to think about sounding out words. Decoding skills need to be learned and practiced so these skills become automatic when reading words. Visualizing (making pictures in your head) helps readers remember what they have read. Good vocabulary skills help readers visualize. Readers can not visualize a word if they do not know its meaning. All of these skills: fluency, visualizing, vocabulary, and decoding are necessary to have good reading comprehension.

Reading comprehension is the goal of reading. Reading is an essential skill for jobs and daily life. Many people enjoy reading and say it is one of their favorite past times. Others read only when it is necessary. Whichever the case may be, everyone needs to know how to read. Learning to read comes easier to some people. Most people need to be taught how to read. It is different than learning to talk. For some people, learning to read can be a very difficult thing to do. But with practice, most everyone can learn to read.

Introducción

Comprensión de lectura en inglés para hispanohablantes Libro 3 se escribió para ayudar a quienes hablan español a mejorar su habilidad de comprensión de la lectura en inglés. La comprensión de la lectura es la facultad de extraer significado de las palabras escritas. Este es un libro excelente para usarse después de terminar *Comprensión de lectura en inglés para hispanohablantes Libro 2* y *Lectura y escritura en inglés para hispanohablantes Libro 3*.

Este libro está compuesto de veinte lecciones. Las lecciones incluyen la práctica de las habilidades de fluidez, vocabulario, visualización, comprensión y decodificación. Hay una clave de respuestas al final de cada lección.

El leer sin interrupciones (la fluidez) es una habilidad importante. La fluidez permite a los lectores pensar lo que están leyendo en lugar de tener que pensar en pronunciar las palabras. Las habilidades de decodificación deben aprenderse y practicarse para que estas habilidades se hagan automáticas cuando se leen las palabras. La visualización (formar imágenes en su cabeza) ayuda a los lectores a recordar lo que han leído. Las habilidades del buen vocabulario ayudan a los lectores a visualizar. Los lectores no pueden visualizar una palabra si no saben lo que significa. Todas estas habilidades: la fluidez, la visualización, el vocabulario y la decodificación son necesarias para tener una buena comprensión de la lectura.

La comprensión de la lectura es la meta de la lectura. Leer es una habilidad esencial para los empleos y la vida diaria. Mucha gente disfruta de la lectura y dice que es uno de sus pasatiempos favoritos. Otros leen sólo cuando es necesario. Cualquiera que sea el caso, todos necesitan saber cómo leer. El aprender a leer es más fácil para algunas personas. La mayoría de las personas necesitan que se les enseñe cómo leer. Es diferente que aprender a hablar. Para algunas personas, aprender a leer puede ser algo muy difícil, pero con práctica, casi todos pueden aprender a leer.

Lesson 1 * Lección 1

Vocabulary * Vocabulario

Animals * Los animales

hawk
halcón

fawn
cervato

goat
cabra

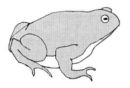

toad
sapo

mice
ratones

seal
foca

rabbit
conejo

kitten
gatito

mouse
ratón

locust
langosta

bear
oso

hare
liebre

Fill in the Blanks * Llene el Espacio

Llene cada espacio con una palabra de la página de vocabulario. Use la figura al final de la oración para ayudarse. Lea la oración con cuidado porque puede necesitar añadir una <u>s</u> o las letras <u>es</u> a la palabra del vocabulario.

1. The _____ make a loud sound in the trees.

2. We can hear the brown _____ growling.

3. I see two _____ on the bridge.

4. The _____ has a mouse in its claws.

5. We saw five _____ in the desert.

6. The _____ like to nibble on our clothes.

7. A _____ lives in my closet.

8. I found a large _____ sleeping under a big leaf.

9. We watch the _____ dive and swim in the water.

10. The _____ play with the ball of yard.

11. Two small _____ have a nest in our garden.

12. My friend has a white _____ for a pet.

Visualizing * Visualización

Visualizar lo que lee le ayudará a recordar lo que ha leído.

Lea cada oración y después dibuje una figura de lo que ve en su mente cuando lee la oración.

In the park, the trees are full of locusts.

The bear and its two cubs sleep in their den.

Fluency * Fluidez

Fluidez es la facultad de leer a un ritmo rápido sin detenerse mucho a identificar palabras. Con buena fluidez, una persona puede pensar acerca de lo que está leyendo en lugar de batallar con la pronunciación de las palabras.

Practique leyendo la historia que está a continuación hasta que tenga buena fluidez.

The Spitting Cobra

The spitting cobra is a snake. It lives in southern Africa. The spitting cobra can spit poison up to eight feet away. When the cobra is ready to spit, it makes a hood around its head and lifts its head. Then it aims at the eyes of its enemy. The poison can make its enemy blind. Sometimes the cobra plays dead to trick its enemies. It rolls over with its mouth open. The spitting cobra plays dead to protect itself. Like most animals, it only bites to protect itself or to get food. The cobra is a reptile and likes a warm climate. It eats rats, rabbits, lizards, frogs, fish, and birds. Its colors range from dull black to pink. When the cobra is an adult it's about ten feet long.

Lea las palabras, primero de arriba a abajo y luego de izquierda a derecha. Practique leyendo las palabras hasta que pueda leerlas sin pausas y a un ritmo rápido.

asking	her	catch
sweeping	corner	match
flying	farmer	pitch
clicking	slower	crutch
playing	farther	hatch

4

Comprehension * Comprensión

Llene los espacios con las palabras correctas de la historia acerca de
The Spitting Cobra.

1. **The spitting cobra is a** _____ .

2. **It lives in** _____ .

3. **The spitting cobra spits** _____ .

4. **When the cobra is ready to spit, it makes a** _____
   around its head.

5. **It aims at the** _____ **of its enemy.**

6. **The poison can make its enemy** _____ .

Conteste las siguientes preguntas en oraciones completas. Cada
oración debe tener un sujeto y un verbo. Comience cada oración
con una mayúscula y termínela con un signo de puntuación.

7. **How does the cobra trick its enemies?**

   _____

8. **Name two reasons why the cobra bites.**

   _____

9. **What does the cobra eat?**

   _____

10. **How long is an adult cobra?**

   _____

Vocabulary * Vocabulario

Llene la tabla con el nombre del animal. Luego coloque una X en cada columna que se aplique a ese animal.

Animal	mammal	insect	pet	has wings	small	swims
1.						
2.						
3.						
4.						
5.						
6.						
7.						
8.						
9.						
10.						
11.						
12.						

Answer Key * Las Respuestas

Fill in the Blanks * Llene el Espacio (page 2)

1. locusts
2. bear or bears
3. fawns
4. hawk
5. hares
6. goats

7. mouse
8. toad
9. seal or seals
10. kittens
11. mice
12. rabbit

Visualizing * Visualización (page 3)

Comprehension * Comprensión (page 5)

1.	snake	4.	hood
2.	Africa	5.	eyes
3.	poison	6.	blind

7. The cobra tricks its enemies by playing dead.
8. The cobra bites to protect itself or to get food.
9. The cobra eats rats, rabbits, lizards, frogs, fish and birds.
10. An adult cobra is about ten feet long.

Vocabulary * Vocabulario (page 6)

Animal	mammal	insect	pet	has wings	small	swims
1. rabbit	X		X		X	
2. locust		X			X	
3. bear	X					X
4. fawn	X					
5. hawk	X			X		
6. hare	X				X	
7. goat	X					
8. mouse	X				X	
9. toad					X	
10. seal	X					X
11. kitten	X		X		X	
12. mice	X				X	

7

Lesson 2 * Lección 2

Vocabulary * Vocabulario

People * Las personas

painter
pintor

farmer
granjero

judge
juez

girl
niña

teacher
maestra

team
equipo

umpire
árbitro

empress
emperatriz

athlete
atleta

boxer
boxeador

fisherman
pescador

coach
entrenador

Fill in the Blanks * Llene el Espacio

Llene cada espacio con una palabra de la página de vocabulario. Use la figura al final de la oración para ayudarse. Lea la oración con cuidado porque puede necesitar añadir una s o las letras es a la palabra del vocabulario.

1. The _____ has twenty students in her class.

2. The two _____ are fighting in the ring.

3. Three _____ can do the job.

4. There is a _____ on the rock near the falls.

5. The _____ are planting soybeans.

6. The _____ shears his sheep in the summer.

7. The _____ shouts, "Strike three!"

8. Our _____ has six girls and seven boys.

9. The lawyers speak with the _____ .

10. The _____ shows the team a new play.

11. The _____ runs five miles every day.

12. The _____ wore a long red gown.

Visualizing * Visualización

Visualizar lo que lee le ayudará a recordar lo que ha leído.

Lea cada oración y después dibuje una figura de lo que ve en su mente cuando lee la oración.

A woman sits on a rock and fishes near the falls.

The farmer shears the sheep near the barn.

Fluency * Fluidez

Fluidez es la facultad de leer a un ritmo rápido sin detenerse mucho a identificar palabras. Con buena fluidez, una persona puede pensar acerca de lo que está leyendo en lugar de batallar con la pronunciación de las palabras.

Practique leyendo la historia que está a continuación hasta que tenga buena fluidez.

Walt Disney

Walt Disney was born in Chicago, Illinois on December 5, 1901. He had four brothers and one sister. When he was little his family moved to a farm in Missouri. Walt liked to draw pictures of the farm animals. In 1923, at the age of twenty-two he went to Hollywood, California. Walt created Mickey Mouse in 1928. In 1937 Walt Disney Productions produced "Snow White and the Seven Dwarfs." In the next five years, they produced other full-length animated movies: "Pinocchio," "Fantasia," "Dumbo," and "Bambi." In 1955, Disneyland in California was opened. Walt Disney died at the age of sixty-five on December 15, 1966. He died of lung cancer. He smoked cigarettes for many years. Several years after his death, Walt Disney World in Florida was opened in 1971 and the Epcot Center was opened in 1982.

Lea las palabras, primero de arriba a abajo y luego de izquierda a derecha. Practique leyendo las palabras hasta que pueda leerlas sin pausas y a un ritmo rápido.

badge	law	join
judge	jaw	oil
lodge	hawk	boil
hedge	dawn	coin
fudge	yawn	point

Comprehension * Comprensión

Llene los espacios con las palabras correctas de la historia acerca de **Walt Disney**.

1. **Walt Disney was born on** _____ .

2. **He was born in** _____ .

3. **Walt had four brothers and one** _____ .

4. **He lived on a** _____ **in Missouri.**

5. **He went to Hollywood, CA when he was** _____ **years old.**

6. **Walt Disney died of** _____ **cancer.**

Conteste las siguientes preguntas en oraciones completas. Cada oración debe tener un sujeto y un verbo. Comience cada oración con una mayúscula y termínela con un signo de puntuación.

7. **What was the name of Walt Disney's first animated movie?**

   _____

8. **Name two other animated movies Disney produced.**

   _____

9. **How old was Walt Disney when he died?**

   _____

10. **Where are Walt Disney World and the Epcot Center?**

    _____

Sentence Anagrams * Anagramas de oraciones

Reacomode las palabras para formar oraciones completas que suenen bien. Comience encontrando la palabra de acción principal (verbo) y luego juntando las palabras para formar frases.

1. bonfire teenagers beach the made at a the

_____

2. need drooping the rain flowers

_____

3. long tall has girl the black slender hair

_____

4. tree pick from girls the will the pears

_____

5. marching a in trombone he band plays the

_____

6. gown princess long a velvet red wore the

_____

7. of books her put locker her all she'll in

_____

Answer Key * Las Respuestas

Fill in the Blanks * Llene el Espacio (page 9)

1. teacher
2. boxers
3. painters
4. fisherman
5. girls
6. farmer
7. umpire
8. team
9. judge
10. coach
11. athlete
12. empress

Visualizing * Visualización (page 10)

Comprehension * Comprensión (page 12)

1.	December 5, 1901	4.	farm
2.	Chicago, Illinois	5.	twenty-two
3.	sister	6.	lung

7. Walt Disney's first animated movie was called "Snow White and the Seven Dwarfs."
8. Disney produced "Pinocchio" and "Fantasia."
9. Walt Disney was sixty five when he died.
10. Walt Disney World and the Epcot Center are in Florida.

Sentence Anagrams * Anagramas de oraciones (page 13)

1. The teenagers made a bonfire at the beach.
2. The drooping flowers need rain.
3. The tall slender girl has long black hair.
4. The girls will pick pears from the tree.
5. He plays a trombone in the marching band.
6. The princess wore a long red velvet gown.
7. She'll put all of her books in her locker.

14

Lesson 3 * Lección 3

Vocabulary * Vocabulario

Places * Los lugares

beach
playa

lodge
hotel/pabellón

barn
granero

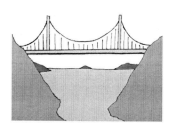
bridge
puente

stage
escenario

shower
ducha

city
ciudad

corner
esquina

cabin
cabaña

closet
armario

house
casa

kingdom
reino

Fill in the Blanks * Llene el Espacio

Llene cada espacio con una palabra de la página de vocabulario. Use la figura al final de la oración para ayudarse. Lea la oración con cuidado porque puede necesitar añadir una s o las letras es a la palabra del vocabulario.

1. You can not park on the _____.

2. Hang your coat in the _____.

3. They live in a big _____.

4. On Sunday, my sister will perform on the _____.

5. We will have a picnic at the _____.

6. The animals are in the _____.

7. My friends go to a _____ in the woods every year.

8. There were large _____ long ago.

9. We will meet at the _____ at eight o'clock.

10. Our house has two _____.

11. Our _____ is the third one from the corner.

12. We will stay in a _____ in the forest.

Visualizing * Visualización

Visualizar lo que lee le ayudará a recordar lo que ha leído.

Lea cada oración y después dibuje una figura de lo que ve en su mente cuando lee la oración.

The farmer milks the the black and white cow.

Mom hangs the skirts in the closet.

Fluency * Fluidez

Fluidez es la facultad de leer a un ritmo rápido sin detenerse mucho a identificar palabras. Con buena fluidez, una persona puede pensar acerca de lo que está leyendo en lugar de batallar con la pronunciación de las palabras.

Practique leyendo la historia que está a continuación hasta que tenga buena fluidez.

P.T. Barnum

P.T. Barnum started the "The Greatest Show on Earth" when he was sixty years old. It was a three ring circus with something different going on in each ring. Barnum was born in Connecticut on July 5, 1810. As a boy he liked to look at strange things. When he grew up he opened a museum in New York. In the museum he put all the strange things he could find. Some things were real and some were not. The museum was a success but he wanted more people to see his show. So he loaded everything onto a train. It took seventy cars and three engines to move it all. The circus would travel to different cities, set up a big tent, and put on the show. Barnum died in his sleep at the age of eighty.

Lea las palabras, primero de arriba a abajo y luego de izquierda a derecha. Practique leyendo las palabras hasta que pueda leerlas sin pausas y a un ritmo rápido.

boat	nice	gem
coach	price	page
loaf	face	large
loaves	space	age
coast	city	hinge

Comprehension * Comprensión

Llene los espacios con las palabras correctas de la historia acerca de
P.T. Barnum.

1. **A traveling show with animals and clowns is a** _____ .

2. **A place that shows interesting or unusual things is a** _____ .

3. **Another word for odd is** _____ .

4. **The opposite of fake is** _____ .

5. **The "Greatest Show on Earth" was a three ring** _____ .

6. **As a boy, he liked to look at** _____ **things.**

Conteste las siguientes preguntas en oraciones completas. Cada
oración debe tener un sujeto y un verbo. Comience cada oración
con una mayúscula y termínela con un signo de puntuación.

7. **What was the name of Barnum's circus?**

    _____

8. **When and where was P.T. Barnum born?**

    _____

9. **What did Barnum have before he started the circus?**

    _____

10. **How old was Barnum when he died?**

    _____

Speech Sounds * Sonidos del habla

Invierta la secuencia de los sonidos del habla en cada una de las siguientes palabras. Diga las palabras al revés. Piense en los sonidos y no en las letras. Después escriba la palabra nueva. La primera ya está contestada.

teach	pitch	judge
cheat		
cash	face	easy
lip	sigh	speak
cuts	snitch	tick

Escriba una oración con cada palabra nueva.

1. _____

2. _____

3. _____

4. _____

5. _____

6. _____

7. _____

8. _____

9. _____

10. _____

11. _____

12. _____

Answer Key * Las Respuestas

Fill in the Blanks * Llene el Espacio (page 16)

1.	bridge	7.	lodge
2.	closet	8.	kingdoms
3.	city	9.	corner
4.	stage	10.	showers
5.	beach	11.	house
6.	barn	12.	cabin

Visualizing * Visualización (page 17)

Comprehension * Comprensión (page 19)

1.	circus	4.	real
2.	museum	5.	circus
3.	strange	6.	strange

7. Barnum's circus was named "The Greatest Show on Earth."
8. P.T. Barnum was born on June 5, 1810 in Connecticut.
9. Before Barnum started the circus, he had a museum.
10. Barnum was eighty when he died.

Speech Sounds * Sonidos del habla (page 20)

teach	pitch	judge
cheat	chip	judge

cash	face	easy
shack	safe	easy

lip	sigh	speak
pill	ice	keeps

cuts	snitch	tick
stuck	chins	kit

1.-12. *Answers will vary.*

Lesson 4 * Lección 4

Vocabulary * Vocabulario

Things * Las cosas

match
fósforo

sticker
calcomanía

patch
parche

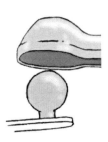

hitch
enganche

crutch
muleta

badge
insignia

boat
bote

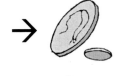

coin
moneda

cage
jaula

gem
gema

hinge
bisagra

pew
banco

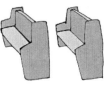

Fill in the Blanks * Llene el Espacio

Llene cada espacio con una palabra de la página de vocabulario. Use la figura al final de la oración para ayudarse. Lea la oración con cuidado porque puede necesitar añadir una <u>s</u> o las letras <u>es</u> a la palabra del vocabulario.

1. **Every employee has a** _____ .

2. **The** _____ **on the door are broken.**

3. **He has two** _____ **on his pants.**

4. **The girl likes to put** _____ **in her book.**

5. **My mother's ring has a big red** _____ .

6. **He has to walk with** _____ **for six weeks.**

7. **We will take our** _____ **to the lake.**

8. **He used three** _____ **to start the bonfire.**

9. **She will buy four rare** _____ **today.**

10. **They will put the sick animal in a** _____ .

11. **The church purchased five new** _____ .

12. **We will** _____ **the trailer to the back of the truck.**

Visualizing * Visualización

Visualizar lo que lee le ayudará a recordar lo que ha leído.

Lea cada oración y después dibuje una figura de lo que ve en su mente cuando lee la oración.

Dad hitches the trailer to the back of the truck.

At the beach, Mom uses a match to light the bonfire.

Fluency * Fluidez

Fluidez es la facultad de leer a un ritmo rápido sin detenerse mucho a identificar palabras. Con buena fluidez, una persona puede pensar acerca de lo que está leyendo en lugar de batallar con la pronunciación de las palabras.

Practique leyendo la historia que está a continuación hasta que tenga buena fluidez.

Babe Ruth

Babe Ruth is a famous baseball player. He was born in Baltimore, Maryland in 1895. His real name was George Herman Ruth. He had a difficult childhood. At the age of seven, his parents put George in an orphanage because he was very unruly. During his twelve years at the orphanage, his parents rarely came to visit him. George loved to play baseball. He played on St. Mary's baseball team. When George was nineteen, the Baltimore Orioles asked George to play for them. Because he was so young his team members called him Babe. After only five months with the Orioles, he was purchased by the Boston Red Socks and played six years for them. In 1919 he began playing for the New York Yankees. Babe Ruth will always be remembered as one of the greatest hitters of all time. In 1919, he made the longest hit ever, 579 feet. By the time he stopped playing baseball, he had hit 714 home runs.

Lea las palabras, primero de arriba a abajo y luego de izquierda a derecha. Practique leyendo las palabras hasta que pueda leerlas sin pausas y a un ritmo rápido.

new	**ear**	**high**
chew	**near**	**light**
blew	**fear**	**right**
grew	**year**	**bright**
stew	**clear**	**brighter**

Comprehension * Comprensión

Llene los espacios con las palabras correctas de la historia acerca de
Babe Ruth.

1. **Babe Ruth is a famous** _____ **player.**

2. **He was born in the year** _____ .

3. **He had a difficult** _____ .

4. **His parents put him in an** _____ .

5. **His parents** _____ **came to visit him.**

6. **He played only** _____ **months with the Baltimore Orioles.**

7. **Babe Ruth hit** _____ **homeruns.**

Conteste las siguientes preguntas en oraciones completas. Cada
oración debe tener un sujeto y un verbo. Comience cada oración
con una mayúscula y termínela con un signo de puntuación.

8. **Where was Babe Ruth born?**

_____

9. **How did he get the name Babe?**

_____

10. **What was the name of the third team he played with?**

_____

Categories * Categorías

Escriba el nombre de cada figura en la categoría correcta.

Animals	People	Places	Things

Answer Key * Las Respuestas

Fill in the Blanks * Llene el Espacio (page 23)

1. badge
2. hinge or hinges
3. patches
4. stickers
5. gem
6. crutches
7. boat or boats
8. matches
9. coins
10. cage
11. pews
12. hitch

Visualizing * Visualización (page 24)

Comprehension * Comprensión (page 26)

1.	baseball	5.	rarely
2.	1895	6.	five
3.	childhood	7.	714
4.	orphanage		

8. Babe Ruth was born in Baltimore, Maryland.
9. He got the name Babe because he was so young.
10. The third team Babe played with was the New York Yankees.

Categories * Categorías (page 27)

Animals	People	Places	Things
seal	painter	beach	badge
bear	umpire	city	match
hawk	farmer	bridge	gem
goat	judge	barn	crutch

Lesson 5 * Lección 5

Vocabulary * Vocabulario

Action Words * Palabras de acción

Coloque las palabras de vocabulario en inglés en orden alfabético. Para hacerlo, escriba primero las palabras que comienzan con a, luego las que comienzan con b, después c, d, e, y así sucesivamente. Si dos palabras comienzan con la misma letra, entonces considere la siguiente letra y escriba la palabra que tenga la segunda letra más cercana al principio del alfabeto.

English	Spanish
1. fight	pelear
2. flew	voló
3. dodge	esquivar
4. fishing	pescando
5. buy	comprar
6. grew	crecieron
7. blew	sopló
8. found	encontramos
9. count	contar
10. chew	masticar
11. draw	dibujar
12. flying	volando
13. crawl	gatear
14. escape	escapar

Alphabetize
1.
2.
3.
4.
5.
6.
7.
8.
9.
10.
11.
12.
13.
14.

Fill in the Blanks * Llene el Espacio

Llene cada espacio con una palabra de la página de vocabulario. Lea la oración con cuidado porque puede necesitar añadir una s̲ o las letras e̲s̲ a la palabra del vocabulario.

1. In the game, you need to _____ the ball.

2. The baby _____ under the table.

3. The wind _____ hard all day.

4. We _____ a kitten at the park.

5. The plants _____ tall in the sunlight.

6. The small boy can _____ to one hundred.

7. Sometimes the hamster _____ from its cage.

8. The boys _____ in their bedroom.

9. Meg is _____ to Mexico on Saturday.

10. We will _____ a new car next year.

11. Tom _____ pictures of animals.

12. Pam _____ gum when she runs around the track.

13. Jim _____ in a jet when he went on his trip.

14. Dad and Tim are _____ at the lake with their new rods.

Visualizing * Visualización

Visualizar lo que lee le ayudará a recordar lo que ha leído.

Lea cada oración y después dibuje una figura de lo que ve en su mente cuando lee la oración.

The hamster escapes from its cage at night.

Meg found a kitten at the park.

Fluency * Fluidez

Fluidez es la facultad de leer a un ritmo rápido sin detenerse mucho a identificar palabras. Con buena fluidez, una persona puede pensar acerca de lo que está leyendo en lugar de batallar con la pronunciación de las palabras.

Practique leyendo la historia que está a continuación hasta que tenga buena fluidez.

The Gold Rush

In 1849, gold was discovered in California. Many people went to California to find gold. The trip west was hard. For every ten people who went west, only two got there. Some died from the cold. Some got sick and died. Others died because they did not have food. Some turned back. Most made the trip in covered wagons. It was like a moving city. People reported seeing wagons all the way to the horizon day after day. For those who got to California, very few became rich. Some people who did find gold made as much as $5,000 in three days! James Marshall's discovery of gold near Sutter's Fort on the American River in 1849 started the Gold Rush. San Francisco went from a small town to a big city in just two years after gold was discovered.

Lea las palabras, primero de arriba a abajo y luego de izquierda a derecha. Practique leyendo las palabras hasta que pueda leerlas sin pausas y a un ritmo rápido.

loud	shark	thank
mouth	yard	prank
couch	scarf	blank
house	march	plank
sound	hard	crank

Comprehension * Comprensión

Llene los espacios con las palabras correctas de la historia acerca de
The Gold Rush.

1. **May people** _____ **to California to find gold.**

2. **Most people went to California in a** _____ **wagon.**

3. **Gold was discovered near Fort** _____ .

4. **People reported seeing wagons all the way to the** _____ .

5. **Very** _____ **people became rich from the Gold Rush.**

6. **Some people who did find gold made $5,000 in ____ days.**

Conteste las siguientes preguntas en oraciones completas. Cada oración debe tener un sujeto y un verbo. Comience cada oración con una mayúscula y termínela con un signo de puntuación.

7. **When was gold discovered in California?**

   _____

8. **Name three reason why people died on the trail.**

   _____

9. **Who discovered gold in California?**

   _____

10. **Name the famous city near the Gold Rush.**

    _____

Sentence Elaboration * Elaboración de oraciones

Expanda cada oración añadiendo información sobre cuándo, qué y dónde. Por ejemplo: *Viento sopló*, se convierte en: *El sábado, el viento sopló y tumbó un árbol en el parque.*

1. **Dog chews.** _____

2. **Boy counts.** _____

3. **Baby crawls.** _____

4. **We dodge.** _____

5. **Girl draws.** _____

6. **Meg buys.** _____

7. **Horse escapes.** _____

8. **Boxers fight.** _____

9. **Dad is fishing.** _____

10. **Bug flew.** _____

11. **We are flying.** _____

12. **Ted found.** _____

13. **Plant grew.** _____

14. **Coach blew.** _____

Answer Key * Las Respuestas

Alphabetizing * Colocar en orden alfabético (page 29)

1. blew	5. crawl	9. fight	13. found
2. buy	6. dodge	10. fishing	14. grew
3. chew	7. draw	11. flew	
4. count	8. escape	12. flying	

Fill in the Blanks * Llene el Espacio (page 30)

1. dodge
2. crawls
3. blew
4. found
5. grew
6. count
7. escapes
8. fight
9. flying
10. buy
11. draws
12. chews
13. flew
14. fishing

Visualizing * Visualización (page 31)

Comprehension * Comprensión (page 33)

1. went		4. horizon	
2. covered		5. few	
3. Sutter		6. three	

7. Gold was discovered in California in 1849.
8. People on the trail died from the cold, from getting sick, or because they didn't have food.
9. James Marshall discovered gold in California.
10. San Francisco was the famous city near the Gold Rush

Sentence Elaboration * Elaboración de oraciones (page 34)
1.-14. *Answers will vary.*

Lesson 6 * Lección 6

Vocabulary * Vocabulario

Food * Alimentos

toast
pan tostado

muffin
mollete

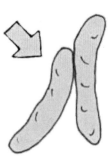

soybean
soja

bacon
tocino

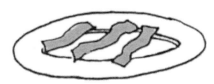

sandwich
sándwich

pear
pera

meal
comida

meat
carne

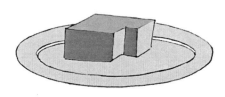

fudge
caramelo

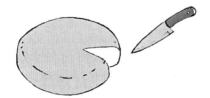

cheese
queso

stew
estofado

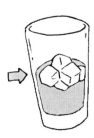

ice
hielo

Fill in the Blanks * Llene el Espacio

Llene cada espacio con una palabra de la página de vocabulario. Use la figura al final de la oración para ayudarse. Lea la oración con cuidado porque puede necesitar añadir una s o las letras es a la palabra del vocabulario.

1. She likes to put lemon and _____ in her drink.

2. He likes to eat _____ for a snack.

3. Sometimes her dad makes _____ on the weekends.

4. When you fry _____ you get a lot of grease.

5. Ed makes turkey _____ for lunch.

6. Dad will use the leftovers to make _____ .

7. Today Tom will buy the _____ at the market.

8. Pam enjoys eating a _____ in the morning.

9. I will have two pieces of _____ with my eggs.

10. We have a _____ tree in our backyard.

11. We ate a big _____ at the diner.

12. Please cut off a wedge of _____ for Sam.

Visualizing * Visualización

Visualizar lo que lee le ayudará a recordar lo que ha leído.

Lea cada oración y después dibuje una figura de lo que ve en su mente cuando lee la oración.

Pam sits under the pear tree and eats a sandwich.

Dad fries bacon over the campfire.

Fluency * Fluidez

Fluidez es la facultad de leer a un ritmo rápido sin detenerse mucho a identificar palabras. Con buena fluidez, una persona puede pensar acerca de lo que está leyendo en lugar de batallar con la pronunciación de las palabras.

Practique leyendo la historia que está a continuación hasta que tenga buena fluidez.

Jin Chuong – A Boy from South Korea

Jin Chuong lives in South Korea with his mom, dad, brother and grandmother. He is nine years old. He and his brother share a bedroom. They sleep on thick mats. At night they roll their mats on the floor. Then in the morning they put their mats in the closet. Jin likes to eat pumpkin soup, fish and rice. Jin rides his scooter to school. Science is his favorite subject because he likes reading about animals. He wants to be a scientist when he is older. At home he likes to read books, play soccer, watch TV, and play computer games. Jin is a red belt in Tae kwon do. Tae kwon do is a martial arts. He is learning Tae kwon do so he can help people, defend himself, and be brave. It also helps to clear and discipline his mind.

Lea las palabras, primero de arriba a abajo y luego de izquierda a derecha. Practique leyendo las palabras hasta que pueda leerlas sin pausas y a un ritmo rápido.

think	thing	trunk
drink	bring	drunk
blink	sling	chunk
sink	swing	bunk
pink	wing	junk

Comprehension * Comprensión

Llene los espacios con las palabras correctas de la historia acerca de
Jin Chuong – A Boy from South Korea.

1. Jin Chuong and his brother _____ a bedroom.

2. They sleep on _____ mats.

3. In the morning, they _____ their mats in the closet.

4. Jin likes to eat _____ soup, fish and rice.

5. Jin rides his _____ to school.

6. Science is his favorite _____ in school.

Conteste las siguientes preguntas en oraciones completas. Cada oración debe tener un sujeto y un verbo. Comience cada oración con una mayúscula y termínela con un signo de puntuación.

7. **Why is science Jin's favorite subject in school?**

   _____

8. **What does Jin want to be when he is older?**

   _____

9. **Name three things Jin likes to do at home.**

   _____

10. **Name another martial arts sport.**

   _____

Words With Multiple Meanings
Palabras con múltiples significados

Llene cada espacio con una palabra de la tabla. Use la imagen al final de la oración o la información en la tabla para ayudrarse. Lea la oración con cuidado porque puede necesitar añadir una <u>s</u> o las letras <u>es</u> a la palabra del vocabulario.

block bloque	block cuadra	trunk baúl	trunk trompa
match fósforo	match partido	seal foca	seal sellar
right derecho	right correcto	light luz	light ligero

1. We saw three _____ at the circus.

2. He won the tennis _____ on Saturday.

3. We will put the boxes in the _____ .

4. Ted ran around the _____ eight times.

5. The small girl used seven _____ to build the tower.

6. I write with my _____ hand.

7. Please turn off all the _____ before going to bed.

8. The big carton is very _____ .

9. He used three _____ to start the fire.

10. He used his tongue to _____ the envelope.

11. I think you made the _____ decision.

12. The elephant sprayed water with his _____ .

Answer Key * Las Respuestas

Fill in the Blanks * Llene el Espacio (page 37)

1. ice
2. soybeans
3. fudge
4. bacon
5. sandwiches
6. stew
7. meat
8. muffin
9. toast
10. pear
11. meal
12. cheese

Visualizing * Visualización (page 38)

Comprehension * Comprensión (page 40)

1.	share	4.	pumpkin
2.	thick	5.	scooter
3.	put	6.	subject

7. Science is his favorite subject because he likes reading about animals.
8. When Jin gets older, he wants to be a scientist.
9. At home, Jin likes to read books, play soccer, and watch TV.
10. *Answers will vary*.

Words with Multiple Meanings * Palabras con múltiples significados (page 41)

1. seals
2. match
3. trunk
4. block
5. blocks
6. right
7. lights
8. light
9. matches
10. seal
11. right
12. trunk

Lesson 7 * Lección 7

Vocabulary * Vocabulario

Cooking * Cocinar

grilling
asar

boil
hervir

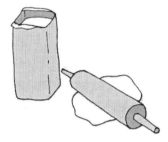

flour
harina

mixing
mezclar

napkin
servilleta

roasting
rostizar

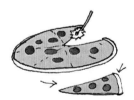

slice
rebanada

frying
freír

spoil
echarse a perder

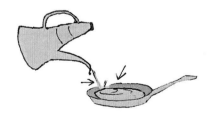

oil (cooking oil)
aceite (de cocina)

blender
licuadora

spice
especias

Fill in the Blanks * Llene el Espacio

Llene cada espacio con una palabra de la página de vocabulario.
Use la figura al final de la oración para ayudarse. Lea la oración
con cuidado porque puede necesitar añadir una s o las letras es a la
palabra del vocabulario.

1. Tom will first _____ the water.

2. Jan will use two cups of _____ to make the cake.

3. Mom puts the bananas and milk in the _____ .

4. Pam is _____ the meat in the backyard.

5. Bill ate six _____ of pizza.

6. Meg is _____ the sugar and butter in the bowl.

7. The kids are _____ hot dogs over the campfire.

8. Put the meat in the refrigerator so it doesn't

    _____ .

9. Please fold these eight _____ .

10. The cooking _____ is in the cupboard.

11. Dad is _____ eggs and bacon for breakfast.

12. Put the three new _____ in
     the cupboard over the sink.

44

Visualizing * Visualización

Visualizar lo que lee le ayudará a recordar lo que ha leído.

Lea cada oración y después dibuje una figura de lo que ve en su mente cuando lee la oración.

The girls are roasting marshmallows over the bonfire.

Dad is frying bacon on our new stove.

Fluency * Fluidez

Fluidez es la facultad de leer a un ritmo rápido sin detenerse mucho a identificar palabras. Con buena fluidez, una persona puede pensar acerca de lo que está leyendo en lugar de batallar con la pronunciación de las palabras.

Practique leyendo la historia que está a continuación hasta que tenga buena fluidez.

Stoves

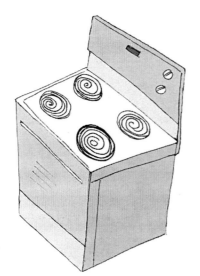

Stoves are an important part of every kitchen. The Chinese invented the stove thousands of years ago. The stove had a place in the middle to hold fire. The Chinese used wood and branches for the fire. Melted iron was poured into a mold to make the stove. It had four cooking holes on top. A hole in the back let out the smoke. Stoves have been made of cast iron, wood, clay and soapstone. Some stoves had chimneys that looked like poles. The gas stove was first used in England in the 1840s. Gas was expensive so only a few people had gas stoves. More people used wood or coal for their stoves. In the 1920s people started using an electric stove. Now people have electric or gas stoves in their homes.

Lea las palabras, primero de arriba a abajo y luego de izquierda a derecha. Practique leyendo las palabras hasta que pueda leerlas sin pausas y a un ritmo rápido.

stove	**pouring**	**poles**
stoves	**hold**	**soap**
pour	**holds**	**stone**
pours	**holding**	**stones**
poured	**pole**	**only**

Comprehension * Comprensión

Llene los espacios con las palabras correctas de la historia acerca de
Stoves.

1. **Stoves are an important part of every** _____ .

2. **The stove had a place in the** _____ **to hold fire.**

3. **The Chinese used wood and** _____ **for the fire.**

4. **A hole in the back let out the** _____ .

5. **Some stoves had chimneys that looked like** _____ .

Conteste las siguientes preguntas en oraciones completas. Cada
oración debe tener un sujeto y un verbo. Comience cada oración
con una mayúscula y termínela con un signo de puntuación.

6. **Who invented the first stove?**

   _____

7. **What was this first stove made of?**

   _____

8. **Name three other things stoves have been made from.**

   _____

9. **Why did only a few people have gas stoves in the 1840s?**

   _____

10. **Do you have a gas or an electric stove?**

    _____

Vocabulary * Vocabulario

Trace un círculo alrededor de 15 palabras que tengan algo que ver con cocinar.

parking	crutch	stove
boiling	slow	lean
raining	raw	coast
poach	carving	chopping
mixing	crawl	refrigerator
oldest	toad	coin
spoil	kitchen	paw
her	peeler	frying
broiling	pitch	bridge
flower	window	thaw

Use las palabras anteriores para llenar la tabla siguiente. Las palabras monosílabas tienen un sonido vocal. Las palabras bisílabas tienen dos sonidos vocales. *Vote* es un ejemplo de una palabra con un sonido o largo. Use cada palabra una vez.

One Syllable Words	Two Syllable Words	Words with the Long O Sound

Answer Key * Las Respuestas

Fill in the Blanks * Llene el Espacio (page 44)

1. boil
2. flour
3. blender
4. grilling
5. slices
6. mixing

7. roasting
8. spoil
9. napkins
10. oil
11. frying
12. spices

Visualizing * Visualización (page 45)

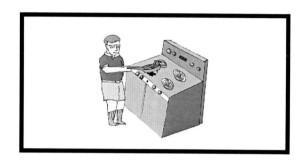

Comprehension * Comprensión (page 47)

1.	kitchen		4.	smoke
2.	middle		5.	poles
3.	branches			

6. The Chinese invented the first stove.
7. The first stove was made of melted iron.
8. Stoves have been made from wood, clay, and soapstone.
9. Only a few people had gas stoves because they were expensive.
10. *Answers will vary.*

Vocabulary * Vocabulario (page 48)

boiling	spoil	carving	stove	refrigerador
poach	broiling	kitchen	lean	frying
mixing	raw	peeler	chopping	thaw

These are the choices for each group.

One Syllable Words	Two Syllable Words	Words with the Long O Sound
her	parking	poach
crutch	boiling	oldest
raw	raining	slow
crawl	mixing	toad
pitch	oldest	window
lean	flower	stove
coin	carving	coast

Lesson 8 * Lección 8

Vocabulary * Vocabulario

Home * La Casa

window
ventana

hammock
hamaca

soap
jabón

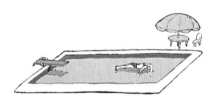

pool
piscina

closet
armario

house
casa

bunk beds
literas

napkin
servilleta

shower
ducha

couch
sofá

stove
estufa

carpet
tapete

Fill in the Blanks * Llene el Espacio

Llene cada espacio con una palabra de la página de vocabulario. Use la figura al final de la oración para ayudarse. Lea la oración con cuidado porque puede necesitar añadir una <u>s</u> o las letras <u>es</u> a la palabra del vocabulario.

1. **I will hang my coat in the _____ .**

2. **Their house has many large _____ .**

3. **The children sleep in _____ .**

4. **We will clean the _____ on Saturday.**

5. **He likes to lie on the _____ and watch television.**

6. **There is no _____ in the kitchen.**

7. **The water in the _____ is too cold.**

8. **Pam likes to lie in the _____ and read.**

9. **We plan to paint our _____ white.**

10. **Is your _____ gas or electric?**

11. **Please put the four _____ on the table.**

12. **He likes to take a _____ in the morning.**

Visualizing * Visualización

Visualizar lo que lee le ayudará a recordar lo que ha leído.

Lea cada oración y después dibuje una figura de lo que ve en su mente cuando lee la oración.

Tim and Meg are painting their house blue.

There are eight hangers in the closet.

Fluency * Fluidez

Fluidez es la facultad de leer a un ritmo rápido sin detenerse mucho a identificar palabras. Con buena fluidez, una persona puede pensar acerca de lo que está leyendo en lugar de batallar con la pronunciación de las palabras.

Practique leyendo la historia que está a continuación hasta que tenga buena fluidez.

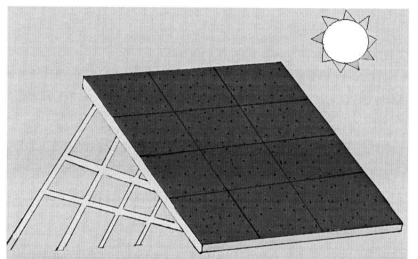

Solar Energy

Solar power comes from the sun. This is an energy every one can share. For hundreds of years people have used wood, coal, gas and oil for energy. Many people, especially in rural and remote areas around the world do not have wood, coal, gas or oil for energy. The sun can be an alternative source of energy. It can bring electricity and water to rural areas. Solar energy works best in parts of the world where the sun shines most of the time. People know how to store solar energy. For example, stones that have been in the sun feel warm. They have stored the sun's energy. Flat plates coated with black paint also store solar energy. The color black soaks up the sun's rays. The plates hold the energy. This energy can bring electricity to remote villages and also pump water to the remote towns.

Lea las palabras, primero de arriba a abajo y luego de izquierda a derecha. Practique leyendo las palabras hasta que pueda leerlas sin pausas y a un ritmo rápido.

pie	light	brighter
fry	high	higher
bike	stripe	dry
slime	tie	sky
cry	lie	drive

Comprehension * Comprensión

Llene los espacios con las palabras correctas de la historia acerca de **Solar Energy**.

1. **Solar energy comes from the** _____ .

2. **The sun can be an** _____ **source of energy.**

3. **Solar energy can bring** _____ **and water to remote areas.**

4. **People know how to** _____ **solar energy.**

5. **Flat** _____ **coated with black paint store solar energy.**

6. **The color black** _____ **up the sun's rays.**

Conteste las siguientes preguntas en oraciones completas. Cada oración debe tener un sujeto y un verbo. Comience cada oración con una mayúscula y termínela con un signo de puntuación.

7. **Where does solar power work best?**

_____

8. **What does the word** <u>rural</u> **mean in this story?**

_____

9. **What is another word in the story that has a similar meaning to the word** <u>rural</u>**?**

_____

10. **Name four sources of energy besides solar.**

_____

Antonyms * Antónimos

Escriba, junto a cada palabra, la palabra que signifique lo contrario o casi lo contrario. Use las palabras de la casilla para contestar.

clean	1. _____	
better	2. _____	
tight	3. _____	
hello	4. _____	
east	5. _____	
first	6. _____	
full	7. _____	

loose
last
worse
empty
west
dirty
goodbye

Synonyms * Sinónimos

Escriba, junto a cada palabra, la palabra que signifique lo mismo o casi lo mismo. Use las palabras de la casilla para sus respuestas.

rapid	8. _____	
rural	9. _____	
scream	10. _____	
fear	11. _____	
store	12. _____	
road	13. _____	
sounds	14. _____	

yell
fright
noise
hold
fast
street
remote

Answer Key * Las Respuestas

Fill in the Blanks * Llene el Espacio (page 51)

1. closet
2. windows
3. bunk beds
4. carpet
5. couch
6. soap

7. pool
8. hammock
9. house
10. stove
11. napkins
12. shower

Visualizing * Visualización (page 52)

 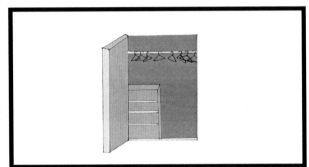

Comprehension * Comprensión (page 54)

1.	sun	5.	plates
2.	alternative	6.	soaks
3.	electricity		
4.	store		

7. Solar power works best where the sun shines most of the time.
8. In this story rural means living in the country.
9. A word that is similar to <u>rural</u> is <u>remote</u>.
10. Four sources of energy besides solar are wood, coal, gas, and oil.

Antonyms * Antónimos (page 139)

1. dirty
2. worse
3. loose
4. goodbye

5. west
6. last
7. empty

Synonyms * Sinónimos

8. fast
9. remote
10. yell
11. fright

12. hold
13. street
14. noise

Lesson 9 * Lección 9

Vocabulary * Vocabulario

Nature * La naturaleza

rain
lluvia

flower
flor

dawn
amanecer

soil
suelo

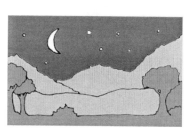

night
noche

dew
rocío

cloud
nube

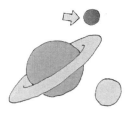

planet
planeta

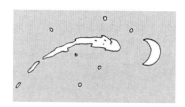

comet
cometa

pumpkin
calabaza

tadpole
renacuajo

tornado
tornado

57

Fill in the Blanks * Llene el Espacio

Llene cada espacio con una palabra de la página de vocabulario. Use la figura al final de la oración para ayudarse. Lea la oración con cuidado porque puede necesitar añadir una <u>s</u> o las letras <u>es</u> a la palabra del vocabulario.

1. Today there are many _____ in the sky.

2. We can look at the _____ through a telescope.

3. The _____ is moist in the shade under the tree.

4. The boy will carve a face on the _____ .

5. The_____ will turn into frogs.

6. In the morning the grass is wet from the _____ .

7. She has many beautiful _____ in her garden.

8. When there is a _____ warning, they go down into their basement.

9. At _____ the sky is full of stars.

10. Last night we saw a _____ with a long tail.

11. Meg likes to walk in the _____ with an umbrella.

12. My dad and his friends go fishing at _____ .

Visualizing * Visualización

Visualizar lo que lee le ayudará a recordar lo que ha leído.

Lea cada oración y después dibuje una figura de lo que ve en su mente cuando lee la oración.

The boy carved a scary face on the pumpkin.

At night, Tom likes to look at the stars through his telescope.

Fluency * Fluidez

Fluidez es la facultad de leer a un ritmo rápido sin detenerse mucho a identificar palabras. Con buena fluidez, una persona puede pensar acerca de lo que está leyendo en lugar de batallar con la pronunciación de las palabras.

Practique leyendo la historia que está a continuación hasta que tenga buena fluidez.

Seals

Seals live in the ocean. They swim in the sea. Seals are mammals. They have lungs to breathe. They do not have gills like fish. The seal's four limbs are flippers. Seals are excellent divers. Seals can hold their breath for a long time. They can stay under water for twenty to thirty minutes. They can dive to depths of 150-250 meters. They come to land or ice to give birth, to raise their pups (baby seals), and to molt (shed their hair). Islands are popular breeding grounds because there are fewer predators around to kill the young. Seals are found along most coasts and cold waters but their biggest numbers are in the Arctic and Antarctic waters. Seals eat fish. The smallest seal is the ringed seal of the Arctic, which is about 1.5 meters long and weighs up to 90 kg. The largest earless seal is the southern elephant seal, which weighs about 3,600 kg and can grow up to 6 meters long. Sea lions are the biggest of the eared seals.

Lea las palabras, primero de arriba a abajo y luego de izquierda a derecha. Practique leyendo las palabras hasta que pueda leerlas sin pausas y a un ritmo rápido.

she	week	puppy
three	weak	happy
eat	theme	meat
clean	teeth	meet
people	sleeps	heat

Comprehension * Comprensión

Llene los espacios con las palabras correctas de la historia acerca de **Seals**.

1. **Seals live in the** _____ .

2. **Seals are** _____ .

3. **They have** _____ **to breathe.**

4. **Seals are excellent** _____ .

5. **They give birth on** _____ **or land.**

6. **The largest earless seal weighs** _____ .

Conteste las siguientes preguntas en oraciones completas. Cada oración debe tener un sujeto y un verbo. Comience cada oración con una mayúscula y termínela con un signo de puntuación.

7. **Why are islands popular breeding grounds?**

_____

8. **How long can seals stay under water?**

_____

9. **Why are seals such excellent divers?**

_____

10. **Where are the largest number of seals found?**

_____

Sentence Anagrams * Anagramas de oraciones

Reacomode las palabras para formar oraciones completas que suenen bien. Comience encontrando la palabra de acción principal (verbo) y luego juntando las palabras para formar frases.

1. gear you car in to need third put the

   _____

2. Saturday complete painters job the the will on

   _____

3. slower the than rabbit the moves turtle

   _____

4. stands catcher the behind umpire the

   _____

5. little after runs fawn the mother its

   _____

6. girl pocket three the new her coins in put the

   _____

7. sleep the at kids bunk cabin the bed in the

   _____

Answer Key * Las Respuestas

Fill in the Blanks * Llene el Espacio (page 58)

1. clouds
2. planet or planets
3. soil
4. pumpkin
5. tadpoles
6. dew

7. flowers
8. tornado
9. night
10. comet
11. rain
12. dawn

Visualizing * Visualización (page 59)

Comprehension * Comprensión (page 61)

1.	ocean	4.	divers
2.	mammals	5.	ice
3.	lungs	6.	3,600 kg

7. Islands are popular breeding grounds because there are fewer predators to kill the young.
8. Seals can stay under water for twenty to thirty minutes.
9. Seals are excellent divers because their limbs are flippers.
10. The largest number of seals are found in the Arctic and Antarctic waters.

Sentence Anagrams * Anagramas de oraciones (page 62)

1. You need to put the car in third gear.
2. The painters will complete the job on Saturday.
3. The turtle moves slower than the rabbit.
4. The umpire stands behind the catcher.
5. The little fawn runs after its mother.
6. The girl put her three new coins in her pocket.
7. The kids sleep in the bunk bed at the cabin.

Lesson 10 * Lección 10

Vocabulary * Vocabulario

Body Parts * Partes del cuerpo

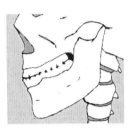

jaw
mandíbula

elbow
codo

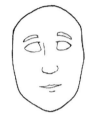

face
cara

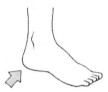

heel
talón

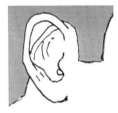

ear
oído

fingers
dedos

hair
pelo

mouth
boca

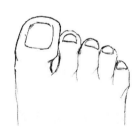

toes
dedos

eye
ojo

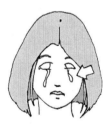

tear
lágrima

joint
articulación

Fill in the Blanks * Llene el Espacio

Llene cada espacio con una palabra de la página de vocabulario. Use la figura al final de la oración para ayudarse. Lea la oración con cuidado porque puede necesitar añadir una <u>s</u> o las letras <u>es</u> a la palabra del vocabulario.

1. **My sister has blue** _____ .

2. **Do not chew with your** _____ **open.**

3. **When it rains, his** _____ **get sore.**

4. **Wipe your** _____ **with this cloth.**

5. **My dad dyes his** _____ **brown.**

6. **In the fight, Sam got punched in the** _____ .

7. **My brother is always stubbing his big** _____ .

8. **I can not hear out of my left** _____ .

9. **Pam has a bandage on her** _____ .

10. **The groom put the ring on the bride's** _____ .

11. **She washes her** _____ **before going to bed.**

12. **Tom has a sore** _____ **from playing too much tennis.**

Visualizing * Visualización

Visualizar lo que lee le ayudará a recordar lo que ha leído.

Lea cada oración y después dibuje una figura de lo que ve en su mente cuando lee la oración.

My brother, wearing the blue jacket, is sitting on the log.

My sister, with a broken arm, rides her bike to school.

Fluency * Fluidez

Fluidez es la facultad de leer a un ritmo rápido sin detenerse mucho a identificar palabras. Con buena fluidez, una persona puede pensar acerca de lo que está leyendo en lugar de batallar con la pronunciación de las palabras.

Practique leyendo la historia que está a continuación hasta que tenga buena fluidez.

Bora Bora

Bora Bora is an island in the South Pacific. It is surrounded by a lagoon and a reef. Many people go there to scuba dive and snorkel. They like to look at the beautiful fish and coral. There are many kinds of sharks and rays that live in the water. Some visitors to Bora Bora have seen the firewalkers. Firewalkers are men who walk on fire. The firewalkers walk on a pit of hot coals with bare feet. The coals are very hot and could burn through thick boots in a few seconds. The firewalkers walk the entire length of the pit. The pit can be up to forty feet long. Then the men walk back again. The men's feet are hot, but they are not hurt. Firewalkers train for a long time. It is very dangerous. Bora Bora has beautiful natural scenery and interesting people.

Lea las palabras, primero de arriba a abajo y luego de izquierda a derecha. Practique leyendo las palabras hasta que pueda leerlas sin pausas y a un ritmo rápido.

snail	gray	make
pail	stray	brake
train	haystack	game
air	subway	made
chain	paycheck	gave

Comprehension * Comprensión

Llene los espacios con las palabras correctas de la historia acerca de **Bora Bora.**

1. **Many people like scuba** _____ **in Bora Bora.**

2. **People can see fish, coral,** _____ **and rays in the water.**

3. **Firewalkers are men who walk on** _____ .

4. **They walk on a pit of hot coals with** _____ **feet.**

5. **The pit can be up to** _____ **feet long.**

6. **They do not** _____ **their feet.**

Conteste las siguientes preguntas en oraciones completas. Cada oración debe tener un sujeto y un verbo. Comience cada oración con una mayúscula y termínela con un signo de puntuación.

7. **Where is Bora Bora?**

    _____

8. **What is a lagoon?**

    _____

9. **What is a reef?**

    _____

10. **What do firewalkers do before they can walk on hot coals?**

    _____

Vocabulary * Vocabulario

Trace un círculo alrededor de 15 palabras que tengan que ver con su cuerpo.

hand	cent	elbow
spine	eyes	pumpkin
badge	gem	heel
few	chin	fudge
shin	spear	face
noise	dawn	cage
flour	nose	toe
seal	leg	east
mouth	arm	finger
ear	toast	hawk

En la tabla siguiente, escriba 15 partes del cuerpo y después ponga una X en la columna correcta de cada una.

Body Part	Your body has one of these.	Your body has two of these.	Your body has ten of these.
1.			
2.			
3.			
4.			
5.			
6.			
7.			
8.			
9.			
10.			
11.			
12.			
13.			
14.			
15.			

Answer Key * Las Respuestas

Fill in the Blanks * Llene el Espacio (page 65)

1. eyes
2. mouth
3. joints
4. tear or tears
5. hair
6. jaw

7. toe
8. ear
9. heel
10. finger
11. face
12. elbow

Visualizing * Visualización (page 66)

Comprehension * Comprensión (page 68)

1.	diving	4.	bare
2.	sharks	5.	forty
3.	fire	6.	hurt

7. Bora Bora is an island in the South Pacific.
8. *A lagoon is a stretch of salt water separated from the ocean by a reef.*
9. *A reef is a ridge of jagged rock or coral just above or below the surface of the sea.*
10. Firewalkers train for a long time.

Vocabulary * Vocabulario (page 69)

hand	mouth	chin	arm	face
spine	ear	nose	elbow	toe
shin	eyes	leg	heel	finger

Body Part	Your body has one of these.	Your body has two of these.	Your body has ten of these.
hand		X	
spine	X		
shin		X	
mouth	X		
ear		X	
eyes		X	
chin	X		
nose	X		
leg		X	
arm		X	
elbow		X	
heel		X	
face	X		
toe			X
finger			X

70

Lesson 11 * Lección 11

Vocabulary * Vocabulario

Homophones * Homófonos

Los homófonos suenan de manera similar, pero se escriben de manera diferente y tienen diferentes significados.

son
hijo

sun
sol

see
ver

sea
mar

sail
vela

sale
venta

ate
comió

eight
ocho

plain
planicie

plane
avión

flee
huir

flea
pulga

flower
flor

flour
harina

hair
pelo

hare
liebre

Fill in the Blanks * Llene el Espacio

Llene cada espacio con una palabra de la página de vocabulario.
Use la figura al final de la oración para ayudarse. Lea la oración
con cuidado porque puede necesitar añadir una s o las letras es a la
palabra del vocabulario.

8

1. There are _____ tadpoles swimming in the water.

2. In spring the _____ bloom.

3. Whales and sharks live in the _____ .

4. The little girl likes to put her _____ in a ponytail.

5. We need two cups of _____ to make the cake.

6. On Friday the store will have a sidewalk _____ .

7. The baby _____ his food with his fingers.

8. The _____ shines in my window every morning.

9. We saw many _____ in the desert.

10. My dog has _____ .

11. There were six _____ lined up on the runway.

12. Their _____ play on the same football team.

Visualizing * Visualización

Visualizar lo que lee le ayudará a recordar lo que ha leído.

Lea cada oración y después dibuje una figura de lo que ve en su mente cuando lee la oración.

The girl put the flowers in a basket.

At sea we saw a sailboat with eight men.

Fluency * Fluidez

Fluidez es la facultad de leer a un ritmo rápido sin detenerse mucho a identificar palabras. Con buena fluidez, una persona puede pensar acerca de lo que está leyendo en lugar de batallar con la pronunciación de las palabras.

Practique leyendo la historia que está a continuación hasta que tenga buena fluidez.

Stingray

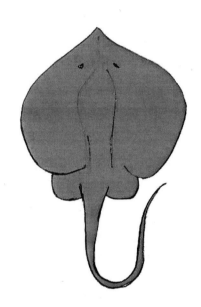

A stingray is a flat-bodied sea fish. Most stingrays live on the bottom of the ocean. They like warm, shallow water. A stingray cannot see its food. The eyes are on the top of the stingray's body. Its mouth is on the bottom of its body. The stingray must find food with its sense of smell and touch. The stingray can be dangerous. By moving its tail around, the stingray can sting anything that bothers it. The sharp spine on its tail gives off a poison into whatever it stabs. At some beaches they suggest you do the "stingray shuffle" when getting into the water. This means you shuffle your feet along the sand when you get in the water. If you are stung you will need to go to the first aid station where you will soak your foot in hot water for about thirty minutes.

Lea las palabras, primero de arriba a abajo y luego de izquierda a derecha. Practique leyendo las palabras hasta que pueda leerlas sin pausas y a un ritmo rápido.

moon	**tube**	**blue**
spoon	**cute**	**glue**
pool	**mute**	**suit**
broom	**chew**	**fruit**
shoot	**new**	**shoe**

Comprehension * Comprensión

Llene los espacios con las palabras correctas de la historia acerca de
Stingray.

1. **Most stingrays live on the** _____ **of the ocean.**

2. **They like warm,** _____ **water.**

3. **The stingray stings with its** _____ **.**

4. **If you're stung, soak your foot in** _____ **water.**

5. **You will need to soak it for** _____ **minutes.**

6. **A stingray is a flat-bodied** _____ **fish.**

Conteste las siguientes preguntas en oraciones completas. Cada
oración debe tener un sujeto y un verbo. Comience cada oración
con una mayúscula y termínela con un signo de puntuación.

7. **Why can't a stingray see its food when it's eating?**

   _____

8. **What two senses does a stingray use to find food?**

   _____

9. **What's on the tail that gives off poison?**

   _____

10. **What's the "stingray shuffle?"**

   _____

Categories * Categorías

Escriba el nombre de cada figura en la categoría correcta.

Food	Nature	Home	Body Parts

Answer Key * Las Respuestas

Fill in the Blanks * Llene el Espacio (page 72)

1.	eight	7.	ate
2.	flowers	8.	sun
3.	sea	9.	hares
4.	hair	10.	fleas
5.	flour	11.	planes
6.	sale	12.	sons

Visualizing * Visualización (page 73)

Comprehension * Comprensión (page 75)

1.	bottom	4.	hot
2.	shallow	5.	thirty
3.	tail	6.	sea

7. A stingray can't see its food because its eyes are on the top of its body and its mouth is on the bottom.
8. A stingray uses its sense of smell and touch to find food.
9. A sharp spine on the tail gives off poison.
10. The "stingray shuffle" means you shuffle your feet along the sand when you get in the water.

Vowel Sounds * Sonidos vocales (page 76)

Food	Home	Nature	Body Parts
pear	shower	dew	elbow
toast	closet	flower	ear
bacon	couch	soil	finger
sandwich	window	rain	heel

Lesson 12 * Lección 12

Vocabulary * Vocabulario

Describing Words * Palabras de descripción

Coloque las palabras de vocabulario en inglés en orden alfabético. Para hacerlo, escriba primero las palabras que comienzan con a, luego las que comienzan con b, después c, d, e, y así sucesivamente. Si dos palabras comienzan con la misma letra, entonces considere la siguiente letra y escriba la palabra que tenga la segunda letra más cercana al principio del alfabeto.

English	Spanish	Alphabetize
1. high	alta	1.
2. higher	más alto	2.
3. highest	la más alta	3.
4. round	redondo	4.
5. bare	descubierto	5.
6. near	cerca	6.
7. busy	ocupado	7.
8. few	pocos	8.
9. drooping	cayéndose	9.
10. bright	brillante	10.
11. brighter	más brillante	11.
12. brightest	lo más brillante	12.
13. entire	completo	13.
14. clear	borrar	14.
15. full	lleno	15.

Fill in the Blanks * Llene el Espacio

Llene cada espacio con una palabra de la página de vocabulario. Use la palabra en español que se encuentra al final de la oración como ayuda.

1. There are only a _____ students in the classroom. | **pocos**

2. The boy is _____ sharpening the pencils. | **ocupado**

3. Please _____ the screen on your computer. | **borre**

4. Many trees are _____ in the winter. | **descubiertos**

5. The plate is _____ of fudge and cookies. | **lleno**

6. They have a _____ light in their backyard. | **brillante**

7. The flowers are _____ in the hot sun. | **cayéndose**

8. The _____ star is the sun. | **lo más brillante**

9. Mom made a _____ layer cake. | **redondo**

10. Tom scored the _____ mark on the math test. | **la más alta**

11. Meg climbed _____ than Sam. | **más alto**

12. The box is too _____ to reach. | **alta**

13. Our house is _____ the grocery store. | **cerca**

14. Fred ate the _____ pie. | **completo**

15. The flashlight is _____ with the new bulb. | **más brillante**

Visualizing * Visualización

Visualizar lo que lee le ayudará a recordar lo que ha leído.

Lea cada oración y después dibuje una figura de lo que ve en su mente cuando lee la oración.

The flowers are drooping in the hot sun.

Many trees are bare in the winter.

Fluency * Fluidez

Fluidez es la facultad de leer a un ritmo rápido sin detenerse mucho a identificar palabras. Con buena fluidez, una persona puede pensar acerca de lo que está leyendo en lugar de batallar con la pronunciación de las palabras.

Practique leyendo la historia que está a continuación hasta que tenga buena fluidez.

Camping

Have you ever been camping? Some people like to car camp. They drive their car to the campground and then set up their tent. Other people like to backpack to a campsite. They carry everything on their backs. They may walk many miles to where they are camping. Their backpack can weigh many pounds. Many people who backpack like to camp in the mountains. They might camp next to a lake. They may be the only ones there. At night they make a fire and cook their food. People who backpack like the peace and quite of the mountains, deserts, or where ever they are camping. Car camping can be noisy. A campground can have many people. At a campground, some people camp in tents and others may be in motor homes. Some people like to play loud music when they're camping. People with motor homes can cook inside on a stove. They can watch television and play video games. There are different ways to camp. How do you like to camp?

Lea las palabras, primero de arriba a abajo y luego de izquierda a derecha. Practique leyendo las palabras hasta que pueda leerlas sin pausas y a un ritmo rápido.

how	frown	south
crown	growl	house
clown	brown	mouth
down	loud	proud
crowd	cloud	round

Comprehension * Comprensión

Llene los espacios con las palabras correctas de la historia acerca de **Camping.**

1. **Some people like to** _____ **camp.**

2. **They drive their car to the** _____ .

3. **Other people like to** _____ **to a campsite.**

4. **They carry everything on their** _____ .

5. **Car camping can be** _____ .

6. **Some people play** _____ **music when they're camping.**

Conteste las siguientes preguntas en oraciones completas. Cada oración debe tener un sujeto y un verbo. Comience cada oración con una mayúscula y termínela con un signo de puntuación.

7. **Write four compound words from the story.**

   _____

8. **Write the three words that are homophones in this story.**

   _____

9. **Name two differences between car camping and backpacking.**

   _____

10. **Name one thing that is the same between car camping and backpacking.**

   _____

What's Missing? * ¿Qué falta?

Complete cada oración. Falta el verbo o el sujeto de cada una de las oraciones. Después de cada oración escriba una **S** si faltaba el sujeto o una **V** si faltaba el verbo.

Ejemplo: _____ run in the park.
The <u>kids</u> run in the park. <u>S</u>

1. _____ escaped from its cage.   _____

2. Dad _____ the salt and flour together.   _____

3. _____ made a huge bonfire at the beach.   _____

4. The boys are _____ apples off the tree.   _____

5. The rabbit _____ in the tall grass.   _____

6. The girls are _____ in the park.   _____

7. _____ is sleeping on the top bunk.   _____

8. The whales are _____ in the ocean.   _____

9. _____ are fishing from the dock.   _____

10. _____ is growling at the cat.   _____

11. _____ is flying in the sky.   _____

12. The farmer _____ seeds.   _____

Answer Key * Las Respuestas

Alphabetizing * Colocar en orden alfabético (page 78)

1.	bare	5.	busy	9.	few	13.	highest
2.	bright	6.	clear	10.	full	14.	near
3.	brighter	7.	drooping	11.	high	15.	round
4.	brightest	8.	entire	12.	higher		

Fill in the Blanks * Llene el Espacio (page 79)

1. few
2. busy
3. clear
4. bare
5. full
6. bright
7. drooping
8. brightest
9. round
10. highest
11. higher
12. high
13. near
14. entire
15. brighter

Visualizing * Visualización (page 80)

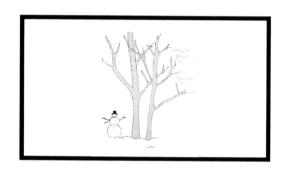

Comprehension * Comprensión (page 82)

1.	car	4.	backs
2.	campground	5.	noisy
3.	backpack	6.	loud

7. Four compound words from the story are: campground, backpack, campsite, and everything.
8. *Their, they're* and *there* are homophones.
9. When you backpack you carry everything on your back and where you camp will probably be very quiet. When you car camp you carry everything in your car and where you camp may be noisy.
10. With car camping and backpacking you can camp in the mountains or the desert.

What's Missing? * ¿Qué falta? (page 83)
Answers will vary except for S (subject) or V (verb). The following are examples for the Subject or Verb parts.

1. The hamster, S
2. mixed, V
3. The teenagers, S
4. picking, V
5. hops, V
6. running, V
7. Tom, S
8. swimming, V
9. The boys, S
10. The small dog, S
11. An eagle, S
12. plants, V

Lesson 13 * Lección 13

Vocabulary * Vocabulario

Numbers * Números

21
twenty-one
veintiuno

22
twenty-two
veintidós

23
twenty-three
veintitrés

24
twenty-four
veinticuatro

25
twenty-five
veinticinco

26
twenty-six
veintiséis

27
twenty-seven
veintisiete

28
twenty-eight
veintiocho

29
twenty-nine
veintinueve

30
thirty
treinta

40
forty
cuarenta

50
fifty
cincuenta

Fill in the Blanks * Llene el Espacio

Llene cada espacio con una palabra de la página de vocabulario. Use el número al final de la oración como ayuda.

1. Meg counted _____ locusts in the tree. **23**

2. The new carpet cost _____ dollars. **40**

3. There are _____ girls in my class. **21**

4. My sister has _____ dresses. **22**

5. _____ athletes were on the field. **25**

6. His uncle has _____ pairs of shoes. **24**

7. The rancher owns _____ horses. **29**

8. The painter has _____ cans of paint in his truck. **28**

9. Sam just sharpened _____ pencils. **27**

10. Today my aunt is _____ years old. **50**

11. Here are _____ napkins for the picnic. **30**

12. The boy grew _____ inches in two years. **26**

Visualizing * Visualización

Visualizar lo que lee le ayudará a recordar lo que ha leído.

Lea cada oración y después dibuje una figura de lo que ve en su mente cuando lee la oración.

My sister blew out the twenty-one candles on her birthday cake.

Tim will sharpen thirty pencils for the teacher.

Fluency * Fluidez

Fluidez es la facultad de leer a un ritmo rápido sin detenerse mucho a identificar palabras. Con buena fluidez, una persona puede pensar acerca de lo que está leyendo en lugar de batallar con la pronunciación de las palabras.

Practique leyendo la historia que está a continuación hasta que tenga buena fluidez.

The Laughing Hyena

Have you ever laughed so loud that someone called you a laughing hyena? The hyena is Africa's most common large carnivore. A carnivore is a creature that eats meat. The hyena's cry is loud and sounds like a howl or wild laugh. Hyenas are related to cats but have feet like a dog. Hyenas live in clans. The clan is under the leadership of a dominant female. Hyenas rest during the day in thick bush or tall grass, in holes dug by other animals or in a den. In the late afternoon they begin their daily search for food. Hyenas are fast, strong, and good hunters. They can run up to forty miles an hour. Hyenas normally hunt alone but will hunt in packs to catch large prey like wildebeests, gazelles, and zebras. In areas where prey is not so abundant, hyenas are scavengers, eating what other animals or people have left behind.

Lea las palabras, primero de arriba a abajo y luego de izquierda a derecha. Practique leyendo las palabras hasta que pueda leerlas sin pausas y a un ritmo rápido.

small	wall	yawn
ball	tall	draw
hall	saw	lawn
mall	law	jaw
call	claw	crawl

Comprehension * Comprensión

Llene los espacios con las palabras correctas de la historia acerca de
The Laughing Hyena.

1. **Hyenas are related to** _____ .

2. **Hyenas have feet like a** _____ .

3. **Hyenas live in** _____ .

4. **Hyenas** _____ **during the day.**

5. **In the late** _____ **, hyenas begin to look for food.**

6. **Hyenas can run up to** _____ **miles an hour.**

Conteste las siguientes preguntas en oraciones completas. Cada oración debe tener un sujeto y un verbo. Comience cada oración con una mayúscula y termínela con un signo de puntuación.

7. **Where do hyenas live?**

_____

8. **What is a carnivore?**

_____

9. **Who is the leader in a hyena clan?**

_____

10. **Has anyone ever said you sound like a laughing hyena?**

_____

Vocabulary * Vocabulario

Trace un círculo alrededor de 15 cosas que encontraría en la casa.

dodge	chair	sea
few	empire	napkin
couch	clock	reach
closet	chin	sink
fawn	draw	spoon
hawk	shower	maybe
stove	drew	lamp
goat	fan	sorting
bed	dish	race
sun	pan	fork

En la tabla siguiente, escriba las quince palabras en las columnas de las habitaciones en donde las encontraría con más probabilidad. Puede escribir las palabras más de una vez.

Kitchen	Bedroom	Bathroom

Answer Key * Las Respuestas

Fill in the Blanks * Llene el Espacio (page 86)

1. twenty-three
2. forty
3. twenty-one
4. twenty-two
5. twenty-five
6. twenty-four

7. twenty-nine
8. twenty-eight
9. twenty-seven
10. fifty
11. thirty
12. twenty-six

Visualizing * Visualización (page 87)

Comprehension * Comprensión (page 89)

1.	cats	4.	rest
2.	dog	5.	afternoon
3.	clans	6.	forty

7. Hyenas live in Africa.
8. A carnivore is a creature that eats meat.
9. The leader in a hyena clan is a dominant female.
10. *Answers will vary*.

Vocabulary * Vocabulario (page 90)

couch	bed	clock	dish	sink
closet	fork	shower	pan	spoon
stove	chair	fan	napkin	lamp

Kitchen	Bedroom	Bathroom
stove	couch	clock
fork	closet	shower
chair	bed	fan
clock	chair	lamp
fan	clock	sink
dish	fan	
pan	lamp	
napkin		
sink		
spoon		
lamp		

Lesson 14 * Lección 14

Vocabulary * Vocabulario

Maps * Mapas

Coloque las palabras de vocabulario en inglés en orden alfabético. Para hacerlo, escriba primero las palabras que comienzan con a, luego las que comienzan con b, después c, d, e, y así sucesivamente. Si dos palabras comienzan con la misma letra, entonces considere la siguiente letra y escriba la palabra que tenga la segunda letra más cercana al principio del alfabeto.

English	Spanish	Alphabetize
1. north	norte	1.
2. south	sur	2.
3. east	este	3.
4. west	oeste	4.
5. scale	escala	5.
6. mile	milla	6.
7. far	lejos	7.
8. farther	más lejos	8.
9. road	camino	9.
10. highway	carretera	10.
11. freeway	autopista	11.
12. coast	costa	12.
13. place	lugar	13.
14. city	ciudad	14.

Fill in the Blanks * Llene el Espacio

Llene cada espacio con una palabra de la página de vocabulario. Use la palabra en español que se encuentra al final de la oración como ayuda. Lea la oración con cuidado porque puede necesitar añadir una <u>s</u> o las letras <u>es</u> a la palabra del vocabulario.

1. We need to go _____ to get to the lake. | norte

2. Our farm is _____ of the city. | sur

3. My uncle's house is five _____ from the mall. | millas

4. We will take the road that goes along the _____ . | costa

5. The largest _____ in the state is on the river. | ciudad

6. Use the ____ on the map to figure out how far it is. | escala

7. There are two _____ that go around the city. | autopistas

8. Mark the _____ on the map where we will meet. | lugar

9. This _____ does not have a stop sign. | carretera

10. The sun rises in the _____ . | este

11. The states are larger in the _____ . | oeste

12. We will need to take a plane to visit my aunt who lives _____ away. | lejos

13. In our state there are several _____ that run north and south. | carreteras

14. You will need to go _____ up the road to get to their house. | más lejos

93

Visualizing * Visualización

Visualizar lo que lee le ayudará a recordar lo que ha leído.

Lea cada oración y después dibuje una figura de lo que ve en su mente cuando lee la oración.

The freeway goes around the city.

He rode his bike on the road that went along the coast.

Fluency * Fluidez

Fluidez es la facultad de leer a un ritmo rápido sin detenerse mucho a identificar palabras. Con buena fluidez, una persona puede pensar acerca de lo que está leyendo en lugar de batallar con la pronunciación de las palabras.

Practique leyendo la historia que está a continuación hasta que tenga buena fluidez.

Travel

Do you like to travel? When you go on a trip, do you travel by car, bus, or plane? Many people travel by car. They get a map to plan their trip. If they are going on a long road trip, they will decide in which cities or towns they will spend the night. They might make reservations at a hotel. If is fun to stay at a hotel because many have swimming pools. After sitting in a car all day, it is fun to jump in the pool. Other people travel by bus. If it is a long trip, the bus will stop at different towns or cities so people can get out to buy their meals at a restaurant. When the bus finally arrives at its final destination, it will stop at the bus station. From there, people will need to walk, take a taxi, subway, another bus, or maybe they have friends or relatives who will take them to where they are going. Many people take a plane if they are going far away. What is your favorite way to travel?

Lea las palabras, primero de arriba a abajo y luego de izquierda a derecha. Practique leyendo las palabras hasta que pueda leerlas sin pausas y a un ritmo rápido.

soon	troop	foot
groom	spoon	stood
smooth	tool	should
tooth	book	would
booth	took	could

Comprehension * Comprensión

Llene los espacios con las palabras correctas de la historia acerca de **Travel.**

1. People use a _____ to help plan their trip.

2. They might make _____ at a hotel.

3. Buses stop in towns so people can buy their _____ at a restaurant.

4. When the bus arrives at its final destination, it will stop at the _____ station.

5. An underground train is called a _____ .

6. Many people travel by _____ if they are going far away.

Conteste las siguientes preguntas en oraciones completas. Cada oración debe tener un sujeto y un verbo. Comience cada oración con una mayúscula y termínela con un signo de puntuación.

7. List three different ways to travel.

_____

8. Why is it fun to stay at a hotel?

_____

9. List four different ways to travel in a city.

_____

10. What is your favorite way to travel?

_____

Venn Diagram * Diagrama de Venn

En esta página se encuentra un Diagrama de Venn. Las personas usan estos diagramas para ayudar a organizar sus pensamientos e ideas al comparar dos cosas.

Vea el Diagrama de Venn. La información sobre Los Angeles se encuentra bajo Los Angeles. La información sobre la ciudad de Nueva York se encuentra bajo la ciudad de Nueva York. La información que tienen en común las dos se encuentra en el centro.

Llene el Diagrama de Venn con información acerca de perros y gatos. Escriba la información de perros bajo Perros. Escriba la información de gatos bajo Gatos. Escriba la información que tengan en común los dos en el centro.

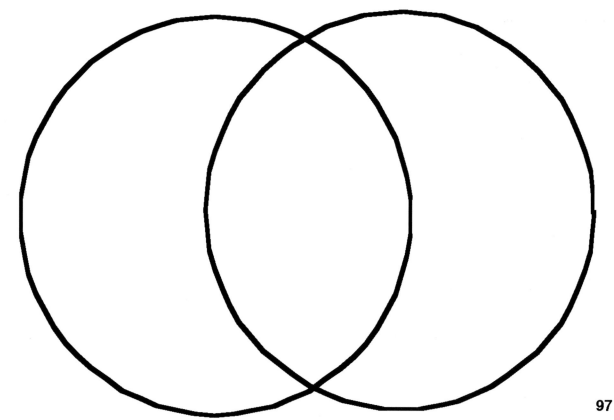

Answer Key * Las Respuestas

Alphabetizing * Colocar en orden alfabético (page 92)

1. city	5. farther	9. north	13. south
2. coast	6. freeway	10. place	14. west
3. east	7. highway	11. road	
4. far	8. mile	12. scale	

Fill in the Blanks * Llene el Espacio (page 93)

1. north
2. south
3. miles
4. coast
5. city
6. scale
7. freeways
8. place
9. road
10. east
11. west
12. far
13. highways
14. farther

Visualizing * Visualización (page 94)

Comprehension * Comprensión (page 96)

1. map		4. bus	
2. reservations		5. subway	
3. meals		6. plane	

7. Three ways to travel are by car, bus, or plane.
8. It is fun to stay at a hotel because many of them have swimming pools.
9. Four ways to travel in a city are by walking, taking a taxi, subway, or another bus.
10. *Answers will vary.*

Venn Diagram * Diagrama de Venn (page 97)

Here is an example.

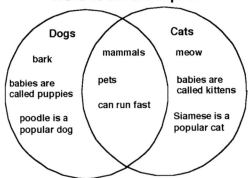

Lesson 15 * Lección 15

Vocabulary * Vocabulario

Describing Words 2 * Palabras de descripción 2

Coloque las palabras de vocabulario en inglés en orden alfabético. Para hacerlo, escriba primero las palabras que comienzan con <u>a</u>, luego las que comienzan con <u>b</u>, después <u>c</u>, <u>d</u>, <u>e</u>, y así sucesivamente. Si dos palabras comienzan con la misma letra, entonces considere la siguiente letra y escriba la palabra que tenga la segunda letra más cercana al principio del alfabeto.

English	Spanish	Alphabetize
1. slow	lenta	1.
2. slower	más lento	2.
3. slowest	el más lento	3.
4. tighter	más apretado	4.
5. light	liviana	5.
6. lighter	más liviana	6.
7. lightest	la más liviana	7.
8. under	debajo	8.
9. smoother	más lisa	9.
10. sharp	cerrada	10.
11. sharper	más afilado	11.
12. sharpest	la más astuta	12.
13. thicker	más espeso	13.
14. smarter	más inteligente	14.

Fill in the Blanks * Llene el Espacio

Llene cada espacio con una palabra de la página de vocabulario.
Use la palabra en español que se encuentra al final de la oración
como ayuda. Las palabras del vocabulario que terminan con <u>er</u> se
usan para comparar dos cosas y las que terminan en <u>est</u> se usan
para comparar más de dos cosas.

1. This highway is _____ than the other one. | **más lisa**

2. On the freeway, _____ traffic stays to the right. | **más lento**

3. The big box is _____ than the small box. | **más liviana**

4. Your new bike is very _____ . | **liviana**

5. My son is _____ in math than in reading. | **más inteligente**

6. The rabbit was hiding _____ the bush. | **debajo**

7. The red shoes are _____ than the blue ones. | **más apretado**

8. The stew with potatoes is _____
    than the stew with rice. | **más espeso**

9. The old man has the _____ mind of anyone I know. | **la más astuta**

10. The small girl is the _____ one in her class. | **la más liviana**

11. He was the _____ one in the race. | **el más lento**

12. The green pencil is _____ than the orange one. | **más afilado**

13. That was a very _____ movie. | **lenta**

14. Be careful going around that _____ corner. | **cerrada**

100

Visualizing * Visualización

Visualizar lo que lee le ayudará a recordar lo que ha leído.

Lea cada oración y después dibuje una figura de lo que ve en su mente cuando lee la oración.

On the freeway, slower traffic stays to the right.

Under a bush, a rabbit was hiding from the large dog.

Fluency * Fluidez

Fluidez es la facultad de leer a un ritmo rápido sin detenerse mucho a identificar palabras. Con buena fluidez, una persona puede pensar acerca de lo que está leyendo en lugar de batallar con la pronunciación de las palabras.

Practique leyendo la historia que está a continuación hasta que tenga buena fluidez.

Komodo Dragons

Do you like lizards? If so, you would enjoy visiting Komodo Island in Indonesia. On this island lives the largest lizards called Komodo dragons. They can grow to be ten feet long and weigh 360 pounds. Komodo Island is a dry, hot, rocky, and fairly barren island. The best time to see the dragons is early in the morning before it gets too hot. The first tour starts at 6 o'clock in the morning. The guides will lead you on a long, hot hike to a dry creek bed where the dragons like to sun themselves in the morning. The dragons detect odor and taste with their long, forked tongue. The dragons move slowly unless they are after food and then they can run as fast as a dog. The dragons hide in brush and wait for a victim to pass. The victim is most often a pig, deer, or goat. Young Komodo dragons spend their first years in trees to be safe from older Komodo dragons who would like to eat them. Komodo dragons use their tails or bite their prey to kill their victims.

Lea las palabras, primero de arriba a abajo y luego de izquierda a derecha. Practique leyendo las palabras hasta que pueda leerlas sin pausas y a un ritmo rápido.

was	**where**	**form**
what	**were**	**from**
that	**they're**	**think**
how	**you're**	**thing**
who	**work**	**air**

Comprehension * Comprensión

Llene los espacios con las palabras correctas de la historia acerca de
Komodo Dragons.

1. **On Komodo Island lives the largest** _____ .

2. **Komodo Island is in** _____ .

3. **The best time to see Komodo Dragons is in the** _____ .

4. **The dragons detect odor and taste with their** _____ .

5. **The Komodo dragons can run as fast as a** _____ .

6. **They use their** _____ **or bite their prey to kill their victims.**

Conteste las siguientes preguntas en oraciones completas. Cada
oración debe tener un sujeto y un verbo. Comience cada oración
con una mayúscula y termínela con un signo de puntuación.

7. **What is the name of the largest lizard?**

_____

8. **How big can they get to be?**

_____

9. **Name three things they eat.**

_____

10. **Why do young ones live in trees?**

_____

Sentence Elaboration * Elaboración de oraciones

Expanda cada oración añadiendo información de color, número y qué. Por ejemplo: *Meg encontró*, se convierte en: *Meg encontró cinco huevos azules.*

1. **The dog growls.** _____

2. **Eggs hatch.** _____

3. **The farmer plants.** _____

4. **The goat eats.** _____

5. **The hawk catches.** _____

6. **The girl buys.** _____

7. **The athlete jumps.** _____

8. **Pam is picking.** _____

9. **Jim wears.** _____

10. **Tom hears.** _____

11. **A kitten plays.** _____

12. **Mark is looking.** _____

13. **Kim won.** _____

14. **Meg parks.** _____

Answer Key * Las Respuestas

Alphabetizing * Colocar en orden alfabético (page 99)

1. light	5. slow	9. smoother	13. tighter
2. lighter	6. slower	10. thick	14. under
3. lightest	7. slowest	11. thicker	
4. sharp	8. smarter	12. thickest	

Fill in the Blanks * Llene el Espacio (page 100)

1. smoother
2. slower
3. lighter
4. light
5. smarter
6. under
7. tighter
8. thicker
9. sharpest
10. lightest
11. slowest
12. sharper
13. slow
14. sharp

Visualizing * Visualización (page 101)

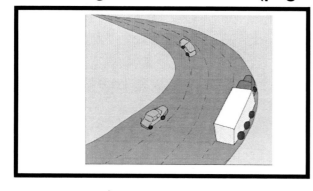 

Comprehension * Comprensión (page 103)

1. lizards		4. tongue	
2. Indonesia		5. dog	
3. morning		6. tails	

7. The name of the largest lizard is the Komodo dragon.
8. They can be ten feet long and weigh 360 pounds.
9. They eat pig, deer, and goat.
10. Young Komodo dragons spend their first years in trees to be safe from older Komodo dragons who would like to eat them.

Sentence Elaboration * Elaboración de oraciones (page 104)

1. – 14. *Answers will vary.*

Lesson 16 * Lección 16

Vocabulary * Vocabulario

Homophones 2 * Homófonos 2

Los homófonos suenan de manera similar, pero se escriben de manera diferente y tienen diferentes significados.

Coloque las palabras de vocabulario en inglés en orden alfabético. Para hacerlo, escriba primero las palabras que comienzan con <u>a</u>, luego las que comienzan con <u>b</u>, después <u>c</u>, <u>d</u>, <u>e</u>, y así sucesivamente. Si dos palabras comienzan con la misma letra, entonces considere la siguiente letra y escriba la palabra que tenga la segunda letra más cercana al principio del alfabeto.

English	Spanish		Alphabetize
1. aunt	tía		1.
2. ant	hormiga		2.
3. they're	ellos están		3.
4. there	allí		4.
5. their	su		5.
6. too	demasiados		6.
7. two	dos		7.
8. to	para		8.
9. bare	descubierto		9.
10. bear	oso		10.
11. meet	reunirse		11.
12. meat	carne		12.
13. mist	neblina		13.
14. missed	perdió		14.

Fill in the Blanks * Llene el Espacio

Llene cada espacio con una palabra de la página de vocabulario.
Lea la oración con cuidado porque puede necesitar añadir una s̲ o
las letras e̲s̲ a la palabra del vocabulario.

1. _____ at the game watching their son play baseball.

2. He was late for school because he _____ the bus.

3. When we were camping we saw two large _____ .

4. I have two _____ that live near us.

5. _____ new house is bigger than ours.

6. The dog found a piece of _____ in the trash.

7. Let's ride our bikes _____ the beach.

8. The girls carved _____ pumpkins for Halloween.

9. This morning there was a light _____ as we
walked to school.

10. _____ are four canteens in the closet.

11. Let's _____ at the corner at noon.

12. There are _____ many rabbits in our yard!

13. I see five large black _____ crawling on your lunch sack.

14. We need food because our shelves are _____ .

107

Visualizing * Visualización

Visualizar lo que lee le ayudará a recordar lo que ha leído.

Lea cada oración y después dibuje una figura de lo que ve en su mente cuando lee la oración.

There were too many bags for the two girls to carry.

At the picnic, my aunt got bit by a two red ants.

Fluency * Fluidez

Fluidez es la facultad de leer a un ritmo rápido sin detenerse mucho a identificar palabras. Con buena fluidez, una persona puede pensar acerca de lo que está leyendo en lugar de batallar con la pronunciación de las palabras.

Practique leyendo la historia que está a continuación hasta que tenga buena fluidez

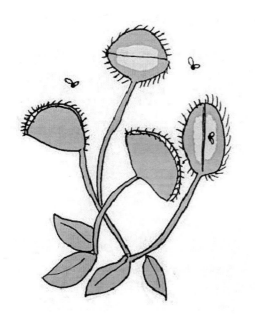

The Venus Flytrap

The Venus Flytrap is a meat-eating plant. It eats insects. The inside of its leaves are filled with sweet, sticky juice. When an insect tries to get this juice and touches the hairs on the plant's leaves, the leaves will shut. Then the insect is trapped inside and becomes food for the plant. When the Flytrap gets hungry again, it will open its leaves to catch another bug. There have been several fictional movies where Venus Flytraps have been large enough to digest humans and eat people in order to survive. In real life the plants grow to be about one foot tall and do not require meat (insects) to survive. Instead they can thrive on sunlight. A Venus Flytrap's life span is indefinite. The trap will die after it has eaten about three or four insects. Most Venus Flytraps live in North and South Carolina in swampy, marshy areas. It is illegal to take a Venus Flytrap from its habitat. The plant was very abundant about fifty years ago but due to loss of habitat it is now not as wide spread.

Lea las palabras de lectura automática, primero de arriba a abajo y luego de izquierda a derecha. Practique leyendo las palabras hasta que pueda leerlas sin pausas y a un ritmo rápido.

girl	come	brother
grill	some	because
bird	they	animal
have	mother	learn
gave	father	through

Comprehension * Comprensión

Llene los espacios con las palabras correctas de la historia acerca de
The Venus Flytrap.

1. **The Venus Flytrap is a** _____ **plant.**

2. **It eats** _____ .

3. **It grows to be about one** _____ **tall.**

4. **The plant will die after it has eaten three or** _____ **bugs.**

Conteste las siguientes preguntas en oraciones completas. Cada oración debe tener un sujeto y un verbo. Comience cada oración con una mayúscula y termínela con un signo de puntuación.

5. **Describe a Venus Flytrap's habitat.**

_____

6. **What do you think has caused the Venus Flytrap's loss of habitat?**

_____

Trace una línea para coordinar las palabras con significados similares.

7. **insects**   **not true**

8. **fictional**   **unlawful**

9. **digest**   **need**

10. **require**   **bugs**

11. **thrive**   **wide spread**

12. **illegal**   **live**

13. **abundant**   **eat**

110

What's Missing? * ¿Qué falta?

Complete cada oración. Falta el verbo o el sujeto de cada una de las oraciones. Después de cada oración escriba una **S** si faltaba el sujeto o una **V** si faltaba el verbo.

Ejemplo: _____ run in the park.

<u>The kids</u> run in the park. <u>S</u>

1. The _____ broke into tiny pieces. _____

2. _____ dropped the fudge on the floor. _____

3. The bobcat _____ for food at night. _____

4. The tall slender boy _____ on the stage. _____

5. Dad _____ pancakes for breakfast. _____

6. We _____ a large footprint at the park. _____

7. _____ ate popcorn at the movies. _____

8. Tom _____ a cupcake and milk for a snack. _____

9. My sister _____ her paycheck at the bank. _____

10. _____ was stuck in the treetop. _____

11. Mom _____ the dog in the bathtub. _____

12. A_____landed on her nose. _____

Answer Key * Las Respuestas

Alphabetizing * Colocar en orden alfabético (page 106)

1.	ant	5.	meat	9.	their	13.	too
2.	aunt	6.	meet	10.	there	14.	two
3.	bare	7.	missed	11.	they're		
4.	bear	8.	mist	12.	to		

Fill in the Blanks * Llene el Espacio (page 107)

1. They're
2. missed
3. bears
4. aunts
5. Their
6. meat
7. to
8. two
9. mist
10. There
11. meet
12. too
13. ants
14. bare

Visualizing * Visualización (page 108)

Comprehension * Comprensión (page 110)

1.	meat-eating	3.	foot
2.	insects	4.	four

5. A Venus Flytrap lives in swampy, marshy areas.
6. *Answers will vary*.

7.	insects – bugs	11.	thrive – live
8.	fictional – not true	12.	illegal – unlawful
9.	digest – eat	13.	abundant – widespread
10.	require – need		

What's Missing? * ¿Qué falta? (page 111)
Answers will vary except for S (subject) or V (verb). The following are examples for the Subject or Verb parts.

1. plate S
2. Mom S
3. hunts V
4. sang V
5. cooked V
6. saw V
7. Al S
8. ate V
9. cashed V
10. Fluffy S
11. put V
12. fly S

112

Lesson 17 * Lección 17

Vocabulary * Vocabulario

Action Words 2 * Palabras de acción 2

Coloque las palabras de vocabulario en inglés en orden alfabético. Para hacerlo, escriba primero las palabras que comienzan con a, luego las que comienzan con b, después c, d, e, y así sucesivamente. Si dos palabras comienzan con la misma letra, entonces considere la siguiente letra y escriba la palabra que tenga la segunda letra más cercana al principio del alfabeto.

English	Spanish		Alphabetize
1. join	unirse		1.
2. playing	jugando		2.
3. know	saber		3.
4. impress	impresionar		4.
5. ignore	ignorar		5.
6. looking	buscar		6.
7. hear	escuchar		7.
8. hatch	salir del cascarón		8.
9. inspire	inspirar		9.
10. growling	gruñendo		10.
11. read	leer		11.
12. picking	elegir		12.
13. heal	curar		13.
14. invite	invitar		14.

Fill in the Blanks * Llene el Espacio

Elija la mejor palabra de la lista del vocabulario para llenar cada espacio en blanco. Lea la oración con cuidado porque puede necesitar añadir una s, es, o ed a la palabra del vocabulario.

1. Jan is _____ the ripe apples from the tree.

2. Jim _____ his book before going to bed.

3. Do you _____ her name?

4. She _____ the new boy to the party.

5. Jan plans to _____ the after school chess club.

6. Do not go near the dog when its _____ .

7. Yesterday the baby chick _____ from its egg.

8. Everyday the son _____ his mother with his singing.

9. The teacher _____ us to do our work well.

10. The cat _____ the playful pup.

11. We are _____ for the lost keys.

12. The boys are _____ in the water at the beach.

13. The dog _____ a sound and starts barking.

14. This medicine will _____ your sore throat.

Visualizing * Visualización

Visualizar lo que lee le ayudará a recordar lo que ha leído.

Lea cada oración y después dibuje una figura de lo que ve en su mente cuando lee la oración.

At the beach, the boys are playing with a large ball in the water.

The cat ignores the playful pup.

Fluency * Fluidez

Fluidez es la facultad de leer a un ritmo rápido sin detenerse mucho a identificar palabras. Con buena fluidez, una persona puede pensar acerca de lo que está leyendo en lugar de batallar con la pronunciación de las palabras.

Practique leyendo la historia que está a continuación hasta que tenga buena fluidez.

AdAmAn

AdAmAn is a group of mountaineers that climb Pikes Peak on December 30th and 31st. At midnight on New Year's Eve they shoot off fireworks from the top of Pikes Peak. This tradition began in 1922 when five men decided to climb Pikes Peak instead of attending the usual social parties and dances. On the morning of December 31st they started the accent up the steep, slippery and windy slopes of Pikes Peak. Hours later they reached the summit house and started a fire to warm their frozen noses, hands, and toes. At midnight they lit the fireworks they had carried up the mountain and built a hug bonfire. Within minutes people from all over the Colorado Springs area noticed the strange lights and fire on the summit. That night was the beginning of a Colorado tradition. Each year they have added one member to the group. Now they take two days to do the hike up the mountain. There are now women in the group. Each year the new member must break trail through the deep snow.

Lea las palabras, primero de arriba a abajo y luego de izquierda a derecha. Practique leyendo las palabras hasta que pueda leerlas sin pausas y a un ritmo rápido.

low	shadow	how
show	yellow	now
grow	bow	town
snow	cow	owl
window	crown	gown

116

Comprehension * Comprensión

Llene los espacios con las palabras correctas de la historia acerca de **AdAmAn.**

1. AdAmAn is a group of _____ that climb Pikes Peak.

2. At _____ they shoot off fireworks.

3. This _____ began in 1922.

4. Each year they add one new _____ .

5. Now there are _____ in the group.

6. The new member must _____ trail through the snow.

Conteste las siguientes preguntas en oraciones completas. Cada oración debe tener un sujeto y un verbo. Comience cada oración con una mayúscula y termínela con un signo de puntuación.

7. **When do they shoot off the fireworks?**

   _____

8. **How many men were in the first group?**

   _____

9. **How many years has this tradition been going on?**

   _____

10. **Would you like to be an AdAmAn member? Why? Why not?**

   _____

Venn Diagram * Diagrama de Venn

En esta página se encuentra un Diagrama de Venn. Las personas usan estos diagramas para ayudar a organizar sus pensamientos e ideas al comparar dos cosas.

Vea el Diagrama de Venn. La información sobre Los Angeles se encuentra bajo Los Angeles. La información sobre la ciudad de Nueva York se encuentra bajo la ciudad de Nueva York. La información que tienen en común las dos se encuentra en el centro.

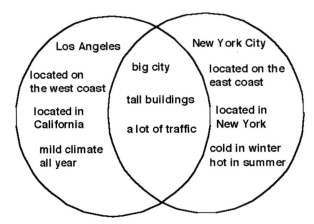

Llene el Diagrama de Venn con información acerca de excursionismo y natación. Escriba la información de excursionismo bajo excursionismo. Escriba la información de natación bajo natación. Escriba la información que tengan los dos en común en el centro.

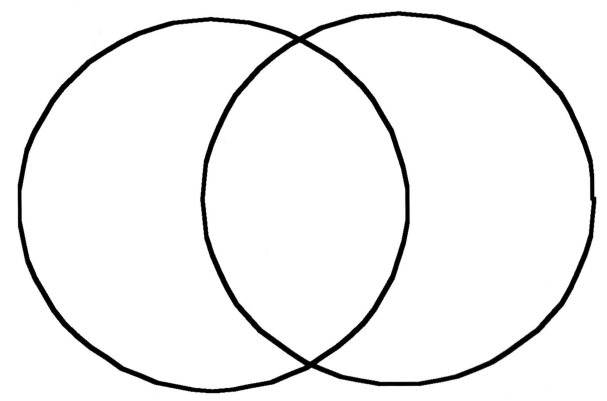

Answer Key * Las Respuestas

Alphabetizing * Colocar en orden alfabético (page 113)

1. growling	5. ignore	9. join	13. playing
2. hatch	6. impress	10. know	14. read
3. heal	7. inspire	11. looking	
4. hear	8. invite	12. picking	

Fill in the Blanks * Llene el Espacio (page 114)

1. picking
2. read
3. know
4. invited
5. join
6. growling
7. hatched
8. impresses
9. inspires
10. ignored
11. looking
12. playing
13. hears
14. heal

Visualizing * Visualización (page 115)

Comprehension * Comprensión (page 117)

1. mountaineers	4. member
2. midnight	5. women
3. tradition	6. break

7. They shoot off the fireworks at midnight.
8. Five men were in the first group.
9. *Answers will vary.*
10. *Answers will vary.*

Venn Diagram * Diagrama de Venn (page 118)
Answers will vary.

Lesson 18 * Lección 18

Vocabulary * Vocabulario

Music * Música

Inglés	Español
1. sound	sonido
2. tune	melodía
3. trombone	trombón
4. concert	concierto
5. inspire	inspirar
6. singing	cantar
7. banjo	banjo
8. tape	cinta
9. alto	alto
10. swaying	menear
11. loud	alta
12. marching	marchar
13. pitch	tono
14. notes	notas

trombone

banjo

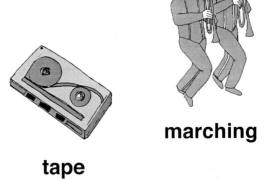

marching

tape

notes

120

Fill in the Blanks * Llene el Espacio

Llene cada espacio con una palabra de la página de vocabulario. Use cada palabra solamente una vez. Algunas oraciones tienen dibujos al final para ayudarle. Lea la oración con cuidado porque puede necesitar añadir una <u>s</u> o las letras <u>es</u> a la palabra del vocabulario.

1. Her son plays the _____ in the high school band.

2. My mother says she can not carry a _____ .

3. My brother loves to listen to _____ music!

4. Here are five new _____ for your collection.

5. The little girl was _____ to the music.

6. I can hear my dad _____ in the shower.

7. The _____ band will play at the football game.

8. Here's the _____ to start the song.

9. My sister often plays the wrong _____ when she practices the piano.

10. Music _____ many people.

11. My uncle plays the _____ and the fiddle.

12. He sings _____ in the church choir.

Visualizing * Visualización

Visualizar lo que lee le ayudará a recordar lo que ha leído.

Lea cada oración y después dibuje una figura de lo que ve en su mente cuando lee la oración.

My uncle plays the banjo at the picnic.

Three small boys are singing on the stage.

Fluency * Fluidez

Fluidez es la facultad de leer a un ritmo rápido sin detenerse mucho a identificar palabras. Con buena fluidez, una persona puede pensar acerca de lo que está leyendo en lugar de batallar con la pronunciación de las palabras.

Practique leyendo la historia que está a continuación hasta que tenga buena fluidez.

Flutes

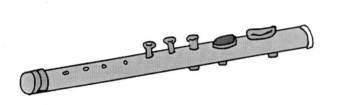

If you have ever been in a school band then you have seen a flute. The flute belongs to the woodwind family. Most woodwind instruments produce their sound using a reed. The flute produces its sound from the flow of air against an edge. A person who plays the flute is called a *flutist*. Flutes have been around a long time. Many ancient flutes were made of wood. They had a few finger holes. Now flutes are made of metal and have many holes and keys. A flutist holds the flute up to his mouth and straight out to the right. They blow air across the mouthpiece. Air moves through the flute and makes a musical sound. The flutist presses down different keys to make different notes. A short flute is called a piccolo. It makes a very high sound. Flutes are played in bands and orchestras.

La primera letra es muda en cada una de las siguientes palabras. Lea las palabras, primero de arriba a abajo y luego de izquierda a derecha. Practique leyendo las palabras hasta que pueda leerlas sin pausas y a un ritmo rápido.

knee	knit	knead
know	knight	gnat
knew	knock	gnaw
knife	knot	gnu
knives	knob	gnome

Comprehension * Comprensión

Llene los espacios con las palabras correctas de la historia acerca de **Flutes.**

1. Flutes belong to the _____ family.

2. A person who plays the flute is called a _____ .

3. Ancient flutes were made of _____ .

4. Today flutes are made of _____ .

5. Flutists blow _____ across the mouth piece.

6. Air moves _____ the flute and makes a musical sound.

7. A short flute is called a _____ .

8. Flutes are played in bands and _____ .

Conteste las siguientes preguntas en oraciones completas. Cada oración debe tener un sujeto y un verbo. Comience cada oración con una mayúscula y termínela con un signo de puntuación.

9. What is another word for ancient?

_____

10. How is a flute different from most woodwind instruments?

_____

11. Do you know someone who plays the flute?

_____

Vocabulary * Vocabulario

Use las palabras del cuadro y escriba la palabra correcta bajo cada dibujo.

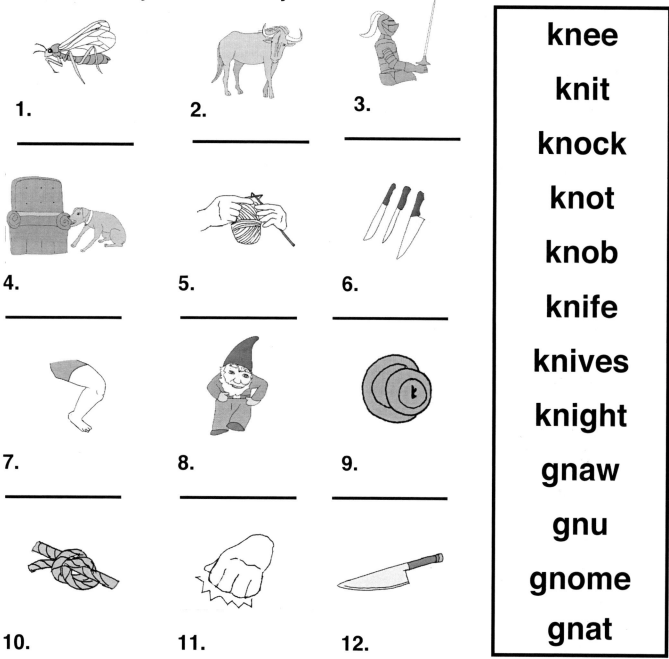

1. _____

2. _____

3. _____

4. _____

5. _____

6. _____

7. _____

8. _____

9. _____

10. _____

11. _____

12. _____

knee

knit

knock

knot

knob

knife

knives

knight

gnaw

gnu

gnome

gnat

En otra hoja escriba una oración con cada palabra.

Answer Key * Las Respuestas

Fill in the Blanks * Llene el Espacio (page 121)

1. trombone
2. tune
3. loud
4. tapes
5. swaying
6. singing
7. marching
8. pitch
9. notes
10. inspires
11. banjo
12. alto

Visualizing * Visualización (page 122)

Comprehension * Comprensión (page 124)

1.	woodwind	5.	air
2.	flutist	6.	through
3.	wood	7.	piccolo
4.	metal	8.	orchestras

9. Another word for *ancient* is *old*.
10. Instead of producing its sound using a reed, the flute produces its sound from the flow of air against an edge.
11. *Answers will vary.*

Vocabulary * Vocabulario (page 125)

1. gnat
2. gnu
3. knight
4. gnaw
5. knit
6. knives
7. knee
8. gnome
9. knob
10. knot
11. knock
12. knife

Lesson 19 * Lección 19

Vocabulary * Vocabulario

Things 2 * Las cosas 2

coat
abrigo

marker
marcador

fringe
fleco

barge
barcaza

basket
canasta

wood
madera

light bulb
foco

spear
lanza

pail
balde

emblem
emblema

carton
cartón

hanger
percha

Fill in the Blanks * Llene el Espacio

Llene cada espacio con una palabra de la página de vocabulario. Use la figura al final de la oración para ayudarse. Lea la oración con cuidado porque puede necesitar añadir una <u>s</u> o las letras <u>es</u> a la palabra del vocabulario.

1. The girl will use _____ to color the picture.

2. There are eight _____ in the closet.

3. Please put the apples in the _____ .

4. Mom will change the _____ in the lamp.

5. Dad buys four _____ of milk at the store.

6. He has a large _____ on the back of his jacket.

7. The men used _____ to catch fish.

8. We need a lot of _____ for the bonfire.

9. Your new _____ is hanging in the closet.

10. The children took shovels and _____ to the beach.

11. I see five _____ in the ocean.

12. Meg will buy the jacket with the blue _____ .

Visualizing * Visualización

Visualizar lo que lee le ayudará a recordar lo que ha leído.

Lea cada oración y después dibuje una figura de lo que ve en su mente cuando lee la oración.

Her new coat has fringe on the arms and along the bottom.

Tom would chop the wood if he could find the ax.

Fluency * Fluidez

Fluidez es la facultad de leer a un ritmo rápido sin detenerse mucho a identificar palabras. Con buena fluidez, una persona puede pensar acerca de lo que está leyendo en lugar de batallar con la pronunciación de las palabras.

Practique leyendo la historia que está a continuación hasta que tenga buena fluidez.

Killer Bees

Bees are very important. Some bees are gentle but do not work hard. Others are mean but work harder. They pollinate more flowers and crops, and make more honey. Flowers that have been pollinated turn into fruit, vegetables, plants, and trees. The killer bee is a hybrid bee. It is a cross between the gentle bee and the mean bee. They do not work as hard or produce as much honey as other bees. Killer bees react to disturbances around their hive. They can stay angry for days after being disturbed. If a killer bee stings someone, the bee releases an alarm that smells like bananas. This smell causes the other bees to become agitated and sting. What should you do if you are stung by a killer bee? Run! Killer bees are slow fliers. Most people can out run them. Run in a straight line and protect your face. Do not try to hide underwater. The bee swarm will wait for you to surface. If you have been stung more than fifteen times or have pain or swelling, go to the doctor.

Lea las palabras de lectura automática, primero de arriba a abajo y luego de izquierda a derecha. Practique leyendo las palabras hasta que pueda leerlas sin pausas y a un ritmo rápido.

again	why	year
house	picture	world
change	much	eye
before	answer	always
follow	kind	head

Comprehension * Comprensión

Llene los espacios con las palabras correctas de la historia acerca de
Killer Bees.

1. **Bees are** _____.

2. **Gentle bees do not** _____ **hard.**

3. **Mean bees work** _____.

4. **Bees** _____ **flowers.**

5. **Pollinated flowers turn into fruits and** _____.

6. **The killer bee is a** _____ **bee.**

7. **It is a cross between the gentle bee and the** _____ **bee.**

8. **Killer bees are** _____ **fliers.**

Conteste las siguientes preguntas en oraciones completas. Cada
oración debe tener un sujeto y un verbo. Comience cada oración
con una mayúscula y termínela con un signo de puntuación.

9. **Why are bees important?**

_____

10. **What should you do if you are stung by a killer bee?**

_____

11. **Why should you not hide in water?**

_____

Homophones * Homófonos

Escriba el homófono correcto bajo cada dibujo.

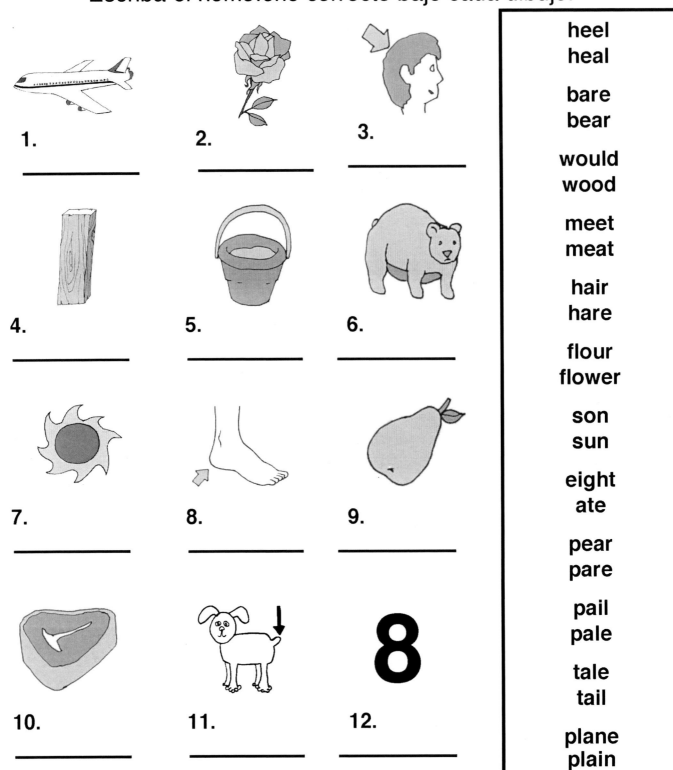

1. _____

2. _____

3. _____

4. _____

5. _____

6. _____

7. _____

8. _____

9. _____

10. _____

11. _____

12. _____

heel
heal

bare
bear

would
wood

meet
meat

hair
hare

flour
flower

son
sun

eight
ate

pear
pare

pail
pale

tale
tail

plane
plain

En otra hoja escriba una oración con cada homófono que no haya usado.

132

Answer Key * Las Respuestas

Fill in the Blanks * Llene el Espacio (page 128)

1. marker or markers
2. hangers
3. basket
4. light bulb
5. cartons
6. emblem
7. spears
8. wood
9. coat
10. pails
11. barges
12. fringe

Visualizing * Visualización (page 129)

Comprehension * Comprensión (page 131)

1.	important	5.	vegetables
2.	work	6.	hybrid
3.	hard	7.	mean
4.	pollinate	8.	slow

9. Bees are important because they pollinate flowers and crops, and make honey.
10. If you are stung by a killer bee, you should run.
11. You should not try to hide under water because the bee swarm will wait for you at the surface.

Homophones * Homófonos (page 132)

1. plane
2. flower
3. hair
4. wood
5. pail
6. bear
7. sun
8. heel
9. pear
10. meat
11. tail
12. eight

Lesson 20 * Lección 20

Vocabulary * Vocabulario

Action Words 3 * Palabras de acción 3

Coloque las palabras de vocabulario en inglés en orden alfabético. Para hacerlo, escriba primero las palabras que comienzan con a, luego las que comienzan con b, después c, d, e, y así sucesivamente. Si dos palabras comienzan con la misma letra, entonces considere la siguiente letra y escriba la palabra que tenga la segunda letra más cercana al principio del alfabeto.

English	Spanish	Alphabetize
1. wear	vestir	1.
2. sorting	clasificar	2.
3. rowing	remar	3.
4. trudge	caminar	4.
5. shout	gritar	5.
6. sleeping	dormir	6.
7. resting	descansar	7.
8. shear	romper	8.
9. reach	alcanzar	9.
10. won	ganó	10.
11. sweeping	arrollador	11.
12. catch	agarrar	12.
13. pitch	lanzar	13.
14. snatch	arrebatar	14.

Fill in the Blanks * Llene el Espacio

Elija la mejor palabra de la lista del vocabulario para llenar cada espacio en blanco. Lea la oración con cuidado porque puede necesitar añadir una s, es, o ed a la palabra del vocabulario.

1. They had to _____ up the hill in the deep snow.

2. The farmer _____ the sheep in the spring.

3. The robber _____ the lady's purse.

4. Pam _____ the ball at the baseball game.

5. The small girl is _____ the front porch.

6. The boy is _____ his toys by color.

7. The children are _____ in the shade.

8. Jane _____ her new gown to the party.

9. Please do not _____ in my ear!

10. We _____ our game last week.

11. If you toss the keys, I will _____ them.

12. The kittens are _____ in the hay.

13. Can you _____ the cans on the top shelf?

14. She is _____ the boat across the lake.

Visualizing * Visualización

Visualizar lo que lee le ayudará a recordar lo que ha leído.

Lea cada oración y después dibuje una figura de lo que ve en su mente cuando lee la oración.

The farmer shears one sheep at dawn.

The boys shouted when they won their baseball game.

Fluency * Fluidez

Fluidez es la facultad de leer a un ritmo rápido sin detenerse mucho a identificar palabras. Con buena fluidez, una persona puede pensar acerca de lo que está leyendo en lugar de batallar con la pronunciación de las palabras.

Practique leyendo la historia que está a continuación hasta que tenga buena fluidez.

Surfing

Huntington Beach, California is known as Surf City. It has eight miles of beachfront, which is the largest stretch of uninterrupted beachfront on the West Coast. If you walk along the beach, you will see surfers. Many surfers like to get up early and surf. They are out by six thirty in the morning riding the waves with their surfboards. They surf in the summer and in the winter. When it's cold they wear a winter wetsuit along with booties for their feet and sometimes a hood for their head. High schools in Huntington Beach have surf teams. The students meet at the beach early in the morning and surf before school. They have competitions between schools. Surfers put wax on their boards so their feet do not slip when riding a wave. You need to be careful with your board so it does not get a ding in it. If it does then you will need to fix it. Every year large crowds gather at the beach near the pier in Huntington Beach to watch the U.S. Open of Surfing.

Lea las palabras, primero de arriba a abajo y luego de izquierda a derecha. Practique leyendo las palabras hasta que pueda leerlas sin pausas y a un ritmo rápido.

tube	**hue**	**chew**
cute	**clue**	**broom**
mule	**new**	**bloom**
glue	**stew**	**smooth**
blue	**blew**	**boot**

Comprehension * Comprensión

Llene los espacios con las palabras correctas de la historia acerca de **Surfing**.

1. Huntington Beach, California is known as Surf _____ .

2. It has _____ miles of beachfront.

3. Many _____ like to get up early to surf.

4. When its cold, surfers _____ a winter wetsuit.

5. High schools in Huntington Beach has surf _____ .

6. You need to be careful so your board does not get a _____ .

7. Large _____ gather to watch the U.S. Open of Surfing.

Conteste las siguientes preguntas en oraciones completas. Cada oración debe tener un sujeto y un verbo. Comience cada oración con una mayúscula y termínela con un signo de puntuación.

8. Write three compound words from this story.

_____

9. Write three words from this story with different suffixes.

_____

10. What do surfers wear on their feet and head when it's cold?

_____

Verbs * Verbos

Use las palabras del cuadro para escribir el verbo correcto debajo de cada dibujo.

1. _____

2. _____

3. _____

4. _____

5. _____

6. _____

7. _____

8. _____

9. _____

10. _____

11. _____

12. _____

fishing

resting

growling

riding

mixing

crying

teaching

grilling

picking

throwing

fighting

reading

En otra hoja escriba una oración con cada palabra.

Answer Key * Las Respuestas

Alphabetizing * Colocar en orden alfabético (page 134)

1. catch	5. rowing	9. snatch	13. wear
2. pitch	6. shear	10. sorting	14. won
3. reach	7. shout	11. sweeping	
4. resting	8. sleeping	12. trudge	

Fill in the Blanks * Llene el Espacio (page 135)

1. trudge
2. shears
3. snatched
4. pitched
5. sweeping
6. sorting
7. resting
8. wears
9. shout
10. won
11. catch
12. sleeping
13. reach
14. rowing

Visualizing * Visualización (page 136)

Comprehension * Comprensión (page 138)

1. City		5. teams	
2. eight		6. ding	
3. surfers		7. crowds	
4. wear			

8. Compound words from this story are beachfront, surfboards, wetsuit, sometimes.
9. Three choices could be miles, uninterrupted, and careful.
10. When it gets cold, surfers wear booties on their feet and a hood on their head.

Verbs * Verbos (page 139)

1. growling
2. reading
3. crying
4. grilling
5. fishing
6. fighting
7. resting
8. teaching
9. throwing
10. riding
11. picking
12. mixing

English Translation of Spanish Directions

Lesson 1

Page 2: Fill in each blank with a word from the vocabulary page. Use the picture at the end of the sentence to help you. Read the sentence carefully because you may need to add <u>s</u> or <u>es</u> to the vocabulary word.

Page 3: Visualizing what you read will help you remember what you have read. **Read** each sentence then draw a picture of what you see in your mind when you read the sentence.

Page 4: Fluency is the ability to read at a fast pace without stopping much to identify words. With good fluency, a person can think about what he/she is reading instead of struggling with sounding out words. **Practice** reading the story below until you have good fluency. **Read** the words, first going down the columns and then across. Practice reading the words until you can read them smoothly and at a fast pace.

Page 5: Fill in the blanks with the correct words from the story about *The Spitting Cobra*. **Answer** the following questions in complete sentences. Each sentence must have a subject and a verb. Start each sentence with a capital letter and end it with a punctuation mark.

Page 6: Fill in the chart with the animal's name. Then place an **X** in each column that applies to that animal.

Lesson 2

Page 9: Fill in each blank with a word from the vocabulary page. Use the picture at the end of the sentence to help you. Read the sentence carefully because you may need to add <u>s</u> or <u>es</u> to the vocabulary word.

Page 10: Visualizing what you read will help you remember what you have read. **Read** each sentence then draw a picture of what you see in your mind when you read the sentence.

Page 11: Fluency is the ability to read at a fast pace without stopping much to identify words. With good fluency, a person can think about what he/she is reading instead of struggling with sounding out words. **Practice** reading the story below until you have good fluency. **Read** the words, first going down the columns and then across. Practice reading the words until you can read them smoothly and at a fast pace.

Page 12: Fill in the blanks with the correct words from the story about *Walt Disney*. **Answer** the following questions in complete sentences. Each sentence must have a subject and a verb. Start each sentence with a capital letter and end it with a punctuation mark.

Page 13: Rearrange the words to make a complete sentence. Start by finding the main action word (verb) and then putting words together to make phrases.

Lesson 3

Page 16: Fill in each blank with a word from the vocabulary page. Use the picture at the end of the sentence to help you. Read the sentence carefully because you may need to add s or es to the vocabulary word.

Page 17: Visualizing what you read will help you remember what you have read. **Read** each sentence then draw a picture of what you see in your mind when you read the sentence.

Page 18: Fluency is the ability to read at a fast pace without stopping much to identify words. With good fluency, a person can think about what he/she is reading instead of struggling with sounding out words. **Practice** reading the story below until you have good fluency. **Read** the words, first going down the columns and then across. Practice reading the words until you can read them smoothly and at a fast pace.

Page 19: Fill in the blanks with the correct words from the story about *P.T. Barnum.* **Answer** the following questions in complete sentences. Each sentence must have a subject and a verb. Start each sentence with a capital letter and end it with a punctuation mark.

Page 20: Reverse the sequence of speech sounds in each of the foloiwng words. Say the words backwards. Think of the sounds and not the letters. Then write the new word. The first one has been done for you. **Write** a sentence with each new word.

Lesson 4

Page 23: Fill in each blank with a word from the vocabulary page. Use the picture at the end of the sentence to help you. Read the sentence carefully because you may need to add s or es to the vocabulary word.

Page 24: Visualizing what you read will help you remember what you have read. **Read** each sentence then draw a picture of what you see in your mind when you read the sentence.

Page 25: Fluency is the ability to read at a fast pace without stopping much to identify words. With good fluency, a person can think about what he/she is reading instead of struggling with sounding out words. **Practice** reading the story below until you have good fluency. **Read** the words, first going down the columns and then across. Practice reading the words until you can read them smoothly and at a fast pace.

Page 26: Fill in the blanks with the correct words from the story about *Babe Ruth.* **Answer** the following questions in complete sentences. Each sentence must have a subject and a verb. Start each sentence with a capital letter and end it with a punctuation mark.

Page 27: Write the name of each picture in the correct category.

Lesson 5

Page 29: Alphabetize the English vocabulary words. To alphabetize, write all the <u>a</u> words first, then the <u>b</u>, then <u>c</u>, <u>d</u>, <u>e</u>, and so forth. If two words begin with the same letter then look at the next letter and write the word which has the second letter closest to the beginning of the alphabet.

Page 30: Fill in each blank with a word from the vocabulary page. Read the sentence carefully because you may need to add <u>s</u> or <u>es</u> to the vocabulary word.

Page 31: Visualizing what you read will help you remember what you have read. **Read** each sentence then draw a picture of what you see in your mind when you read the sentence.

Page 32: Fluency is the ability to read at a fast pace without stopping much to identify words. With good fluency, a person can think about what he/she is reading instead of struggling with sounding out words. **Practice** reading the story below until you have good fluency. **Read** the words, first going down the columns and then across. Practice reading the words until you can read them smoothly and at a fast pace.

Page 33: Fill in the blanks with the correct words from the story about *The Gold Rush*. **Answer** the following questions in complete sentences. Each sentence must have a subject and a verb. Start each sentence with a capital letter and end it with a punctuation mark.

Page 34: Expand each sentence by adding when, what and where information. For example: *Wind blew.* becomes *On Saturday, the wind blew a tree over in the park.*

Lesson 6

Page 37: Fill in each blank with a word from the vocabulary page. Use the picture at the end of the sentence to help you. Read the sentence carefully because you may need to add <u>s</u> or <u>es</u> to the vocabulary word.

Page 38: Visualizing what you read will help you remember what you have read. **Read** each sentence then draw a picture of what you see in your mind when you read the sentence.

Page 39: Fluency is the ability to read at a fast pace without stopping much to identify words. With good fluency, a person can think about what he/she is reading instead of struggling with sounding out words. **Practice** reading the story below until you have good fluency. **Read** the words, first going down the columns and then across. Practice reading the words until you can read them smoothly and at a fast pace.

Page 40: Fill in the blanks with the correct words from the story about *Jin Chuong – A Boy from South Korea*. **Answer** the following questions in complete sentences. Each sentence must have a subject and a verb. Start each sentence with a capital letter and end it with a punctuation mark.

Page 41: Fill in each blank with a word from the chart. Use the picture at the end of the sentence or the information in the chart to help you. Read the sentence carefully because you may need to add <u>s</u> or <u>es</u> to the word.

Lesson 7

Page 44: Fill in each blank with a word from the vocabulary page. Use the picture at the end of the sentence to help you. Read the sentence carefully because you may need to add s or es to the vocabulary word.

Page 45: Visualizing what you read will help you remember what you have read. **Read** each sentence then draw a picture of what you see in your mind when you read the sentence.

Page 46: Fluency is the ability to read at a fast pace without stopping much to identify words. With good fluency, a person can think about what he/she is reading instead of struggling with sounding out words. **Practice** reading the story below until you have good fluency. **Read** the words, first going down the columns and then across. Practice reading the words until you can read them smoothly and at a fast pace.

Page 47: Fill in the blanks with the correct words from the story about *Stoves*. **Answer** the following questions in complete sentences. Each sentence must have a subject and a verb. Start each sentence with a capital letter and end it with a punctuation mark.

Page 48: Draw a circle around 15 words that have something to do with cooking. **Use** words from above to fill in the chart below. One syllable words have one vowel sound. Two syllable words have two vowel sounds. *Vote* is an example of a word with the long o sound. Use each word once.

Lesson 8

Page 51: Fill in each blank with a word from the vocabulary page. Use the picture at the end of the sentence to help you. Read the sentence carefully because you may need to add s or es to the vocabulary word.

Page 52: Visualizing what you read will help you remember what you have read. **Read** each sentence then draw a picture of what you see in your mind when you read the sentence.

Page 53: Fluency is the ability to read at a fast pace without stopping much to identify words. With good fluency, a person can think about what he/she is reading instead of struggling with sounding out words. **Practice** reading the story below until you have good fluency. **Read** the words, first going down the columns and then across. Practice reading the words until you can read them smoothly and at a fast pace.

Page 54: Fill in the blanks with the correct words from the story about *Solar Energy*. **Answer** the following questions in complete sentences. Each sentence must have a subject and a verb. Start each sentence with a capital letter and end it with a punctuation mark.

Page 55: Next to each word, write the word that means the opposite or almost the opposite. Use the words in the box for your answers. **Next** to each word, write the word that means the same or almost the same. Use the words in the box for your answers.

Lesson 9

Page 58: Fill in each blank with a word from the vocabulary page. Use the picture at the end of the sentence to help you. Read the sentence carefully because you may need to add s or es to the vocabulary word.

Page 59: Visualizing what you read will help you remember what you have read. Read each sentence then draw a picture of what you see in your mind when you read the sentence.

Page 60: Fluency is the ability to read at a fast pace without stopping much to identify words. With good fluency, a person can think about what he/she is reading instead of struggling with sounding out words. **Practice** reading the story below until you have good fluency. **Read** the words, first going down the columns and then across. Practice reading the words until you can read them smoothly and at a fast pace.

Page 61: Fill in the blanks with the correct words from the story about *Seals*. **Answer** the following questions in complete sentences. Each sentence must have a subject and a verb. Start each sentence with a capital letter and end it with a punctuation mark.

Page 62: Rearrange the words to make a complete sentence. Start by finding the main action word (verb) and then putting words together to make phrases.

Lesson 10

Page 65: Fill in each blank with a word from the vocabulary page. Use the picture at the end of the sentence to help you. Read the sentence carefully because you may need to add s or es to the vocabulary word.

Page 66: Visualizing what you read will help you remember what you have read. **Read** each sentence then draw a picture of what you see in your mind when you read the sentence.

Page 67: Fluency is the ability to read at a fast pace without stopping much to identify words. With good fluency, a person can think about what he/she is reading instead of struggling with sounding out words. **Practice** reading the story below until you have good fluency. **Read** the words, first going down the columns and then across. Practice reading the words until you can read them smoothly and at a fast pace.

Page 68: Fill in the blanks with the correct words from the story about *Bora Bora*. **Answer** the following questions in complete sentences. Each sentence must have a subject and a verb. Start each sentence with a capital letter and end it with a punctuation mark.

Page 69: Draw a circle around 15 words that has something to do with your body. **In** the chart below, write in 15 body parts from above and then put an X in the correct column for each one.

Lesson 11

Page 71: Homophones are words that sound alike, but are spelled differently and have different meanings.

Page 72: Fill in each blank with a word from the vocabulary page. Use the picture at the end of the sentence to help you. Read the sentence carefully because you may need to add s or es to the vocabulary word.

Page 73: Visualizing what you read will help you remember what you have read. **Read** each sentence then draw a picture of what you see in your mind when you read the sentence.

Page 74: Fluency is the ability to read at a fast pace without stopping much to identify words. With good fluency, a person can think about what he/she is reading instead of struggling with sounding out words. **Practice** reading the story below until you have good fluency. **Read** the words, first going down the columns and then across. Practice reading the words until you can read them smoothly and at a fast pace.

Page 75: Fill in the blanks with the correct words from the story about *Stingray*. **Answer** the following questions in complete sentences. Each sentence must have a subject and a verb. Start each sentence with a capital letter and end it with a punctuation mark.

Page 76: Write the name of each picture in the correct category.

Lesson 12

Page 78: Alphabetize the English vocabulary words. To alphabetize, write all the a words first, then the b, then c, d, e, and so forth. If two words begin with the same letter then look at the next letter and write the word which has the second letter closest to the beginning of the alphabet.

Page 79: Fill in each blank with a word from the vocabulary page. Use the Spanish word at the end of the sentence to help you.

Page 80: Visualizing what you read will help you remember what you have read. **Read** each sentence then draw a picture of what you see in your mind when you read the sentence.

Page 81: Fluency is the ability to read at a fast pace without stopping much to identify words. With good fluency, a person can think about what he/she is reading instead of struggling with sounding out words. **Practice** reading the story below until you have good fluency. **Read** the words, first going down the columns and then across. Practice reading the words until you can read them smoothly and at a fast pace.

Page 82: Fill in the blanks with the correct words from the story about *Camping*. **Answer** the following questions in complete sentences. Each sentence must have a subject and a verb. Start each sentence with a capital letter and end it with a punctuation mark.

Page 83: Complete each sentence. The verb or subject part of the sentence is missing. After each sentence write **S** if the subject was missing or **V** if the verb was missing.

Example: _____ run in the park.

The kids run in the park.   S

146

Lesson 13

Page 86: Fill in each blank with a word from the vocabulary page. Use the number at the end of the sentence to help you.

Page 87: Visualizing what you read will help you remember what you have read. **Read** each sentence then draw a picture of what you see in your mind when you read the sentence.

Page 88: Fluency is the ability to read at a fast pace without stopping much to identify words. With good fluency, a person can think about what he/she is reading instead of struggling with sounding out words. **Practice** reading the story below until you have good fluency. **Read** the words, first going down the columns and then across. Practice reading the words until you can read them smoothly and at a fast pace.

Page 89: Fill in the blanks with the correct words from the story about *The Laughing Hyena*. **Answer** the following questions in complete sentences. Each sentence must have a subject and a verb. Start each sentence with a capital letter and end it with a punctuation mark.

Page 90: Draw a circle around 15 things that you would find at home. **In** the chart below, write in the fifteen things under the rooms where you would most likely find them. You may write a word more than once.

Lesson 14

Page 92: Alphabetize the English vocabulary words. To alphabetize, write all the <u>a</u> words first, then the <u>b</u>, then <u>c</u>, <u>d</u>, <u>e</u>, and so forth. If two words begin with the same letter then look at the next letter and write the word which has the second letter closest to the beginning of the alphabet.

Page 93: Fill in each blank with a word from the vocabulary page. Use the Spanish word at the end of the sentence to help you. Read the sentence carefully because you may need to add <u>s</u> or <u>es</u> to the vocabulary word.

Page 94: Visualizing what you read will help you remember what you have read. **Read** each sentence then draw a picture of what you see in your mind when you read the sentence.

Page 95: Fluency is the ability to read at a fast pace without stopping much to identify words. With good fluency, a person can think about what he/she is reading instead of struggling with sounding out words. **Practice** reading the story below until you have good fluency. **Read** the words, first going down the columns and then across. Practice reading the words until you can read them smoothly and at a fast pace.

Page 96: Fill in the blanks with the correct words from the story about *Travel*. **Answer** the following questions in complete sentences. Each sentence must have a subject and a verb. Start each sentence with a capital letter and end it with a punctuation mark.

Page 97: Look at the Venn Diagram. Information about Los Angeles is under Los Angeles. Information about New York City is under New York City. Information that they both have in common is in the middle. **Fill** in the Venn Diagram with information about Dogs and

Lesson 15

Page 99: Alphabetize the English vocabulary words. To alphabetize, write all the <u>a</u> words first, then the <u>b</u>, then <u>c</u>, <u>d</u>, <u>e</u>, and so forth. If two words begin with the same letter then look at the next letter and write the word which has the second letter closest to the beginning of the alphabet.

Page 100: Fill in each blank with a word from the vocabulary page. Use the Spanish word at the end of the sentence to help you. The vocabulary words ending in <u>er</u> are used when comparing two things and the ones ending with <u>est</u> are used when comparing more than two things.

Page 101: Visualizing what you read will help you remember what you have read. Read each sentence then draw a picture of what you see in your mind when you read the sentence.

Page 102: Fluency is the ability to read at a fast pace without stopping much to identify words. With good fluency, a person can think about what he/she is reading instead of struggling with sounding out words. **Practice** reading the story below until you have good fluency. **Read** the words, first going down the columns and then across. Practice reading the words until you can read them smoothly and at a fast pace.

Page 103: Fill in the blanks with the correct words from the story about *Komodo Dragons*. **Answer** the following questions in complete sentences. Each sentence must have a subject and a verb. Start each sentence with a capital letter and end it with a punctuation mark.

Page 104: Expand each sentence by adding color, number and what information. For example: *Meg found.* becomes *Meg found five blue eggs.*

Lesson 16

Page 106: Homophones are words that sound alike, but are spelled differently and have different meanings. **Alphabetize** the English vocabulary words. To alphabetize, write all the <u>a</u> words first, then the <u>b</u>, then <u>c</u>, <u>d</u>, <u>e</u>, and so forth. If two words begin with the same letter then look at the next letter and write the word which has the second letter closest to the beginning of the alphabet.

Page 107: Fill in each blank with a word from the vocabulary page. Read the sentence carefully because you may need to add <u>s</u> or <u>es</u> to the vocabulary word.

Page 108: Visualizing what you read will help you remember what you have read. **Read** each sentence then draw a picture of what you see in your mind when you read the sentence.

Page 109: Fluency is the ability to read at a fast pace without stopping much to identify words. With good fluency, a person can think about what he/she is reading instead of struggling with sounding out words. **Practice** reading the story below until you have good fluency. **Read** the words, first going down the columns and then across. Practice reading the words until you can read them smoothly and at a fast pace.

Page 110: Fill in the blanks with the correct words from the story about *The Venus Flytrap*. **Answer** the following questions in complete sentences. Each sentence must have a subject and a verb. Start each sentence with a capital letter and end it with a punctuation mark. **Draw** a line to match the words with similar meanings.

Page 111: Complete each sentence. The verb or subject part of the sentence is missing. After each sentence write **S** if the subject was missing or **V** if the verb was missing.

Example: _____ run in the park.

The kids run in the park.   S

Lesson 17

Page 113: Alphabetize the English vocabulary words. To alphabetize, write all the <u>a</u> words first, then the <u>b</u>, then <u>c</u>, <u>d</u>, <u>e</u>, and so forth. If two words begin with the same letter then look at the next letter and write the word which has the second letter closest to the beginning of the alphabet.

Page 114: Choose the best word from the vocabulary list to fill in each blank. Read the sentence carefully because you may need to add <u>s</u>, <u>es</u> or <u>ed</u> to the vocabulary word.

Page 115: Visualizing what you read will help you remember what you have read. **Read** each sentence then draw a picture of what you see in your mind when you read the sentence.

Page 116: Fluency is the ability to read at a fast pace without stopping much to identify words. With good fluency, a person can think about what he/she is reading instead of struggling with sounding out words. **Practice** reading the story below until you have good fluency. **Read** the words, first going down the columns and then across. Practice reading the words until you can read them smoothly and at a fast pace.

Page 117: Fill in the blanks with the correct words from the story about *AdAmAn*. **Answer** the following questions in complete sentences. Each sentence must have a subject and a verb. Start each sentence with a capital letter and end it with a punctuation mark.

Page 118: On this page is a Venn diagram. People use Venn Diagrams to help organize their thoughts and ideas when comparing two things. **Look** at the Venn Diagram. Information about Los Angeles is under Los Angeles. Information about New York City is under New York City. Information that they both have in common is in the middle. **Fill** in the Venn Diagram with information about Hiking and Swimming. Write information about hiking under Hiking. Write information about swimming under Swimming. Write information that they both have in common in the middle.

Lesson 18

Page 121: Fill in each blank with a word from the vocabulary page. Use each word once. Some sentence have pictures at the end to help you. Read the sentence carefully because you may need to add <u>s</u> or <u>es</u> to the vocabulary word.

Page 122: Visualizing what you read will help you remember what you have read. **Read** each sentence then draw a picture of what you see in your mind when you read the sentence.

Page 123: Fluency is the ability to read at a fast pace without stopping much to identify words. With good fluency, a person can think about what he/she is reading instead of struggling with sounding out words. **Practice** reading the story below until you have good fluency. **The** first letter is silent in each of the following words. Read the words, first going down the columns and then across. Practice reading the words until you can read them smoothly and at a fast pace.

Page 124: Fill in the blanks with the correct words from the story about *Flutes*. **Answer** the following questions in complete sentences. Each sentence must have a subject and a verb. Start each sentence with a capital letter and end it with a punctuation mark.

Page 125: Use the words in the box and write the correct word under each picture. **On** another piece of paper write a sentence with each word.

Lesson 19

Page 128: Fill in each blank with a word from the vocabulary page. Use the picture at the end of the sentence to help you. Read the sentence carefully because you may need to add s or es to the vocabulary word.

Page 129: Visualizing what you read will help you remember what you have read. **Read** each sentence then draw a picture of what you see in your mind when you read the sentence.

Page 130: Fluency is the ability to read at a fast pace without stopping much to identify words. With good fluency, a person can think about what he/she is reading instead of struggling with sounding out words. **Practice** reading the story below until you have good fluency. **Read** the words, first going down the columns and then across. Practice reading the words until you can read them smoothly and at a fast pace.

Page 131: Fill in the blanks with the correct words from the story about *Killer Bees*. **Answer** the following questions in complete sentences. Each sentence must have a subject and a verb. Start each sentence with a capital letter and end it with a punctuation mark.

Page 132: Write the correct homophone under each picture. **On** another piece of paper write a sentence with each homophone that you did not use.

Lesson 20

Page 134: Alphabetize the English vocabulary words. To alphabetize, write all the a words first, then the b, then c, d, e, and so forth. If two words begin with the same letter then look at the next letter and write the word which has the second letter closest to the beginning of the alphabet.

Page 135: Fill in each blank with a word from the vocabulary page. Use the picture at the end of the sentence to help you. Read the sentence carefully because you may need to add s, es or ed to the vocabulary word.

Page 136: Visualizing what you read will help you remember what you have read. **Read** each sentence then draw a picture of what you see in your mind when you read the sentence.

Page 137: Fluency is the ability to read at a fast pace without stopping much to identify words. With good fluency, a person can think about what he/she is reading instead of struggling with sounding out words. **Practice** reading the story below until you have good fluency. **Read** the words, first going down the columns and then across. Practice reading the words until you can read them smoothly and at a fast pace.

Page 138: Fill in the blanks with the correct words from the story about *Surfing*. **Answer** the following questions in complete sentences. Each sentence must have a subject and a verb. Start each sentence with a capital letter and end it with a punctuation mark.

Page 139: Use the words in the box to write the correct verb under each picture. **On** another piece of paper write a sentence with each word.

Índice

Index

Books Available From **FISHER HILL**
For Ages 10-Adult

ENGLISH READING COMPREHENSION FOR THE SPANISH SPEAKER Book 1, 2 & 3

ENGLISH READING AND SPELLING FOR THE SPANISH SPEAKER Books 1, 2, 3, 4, 5 & 6

ENGLISH for the SPANISH SPEAKER Books 1, 2, 3, 4 & Cassettes

SPANISH made FUN and EASY Books 1 & 2

HEALTH Easy to Read

UNITED STATES OF AMERICA Stories, Maps, Activities in Spanish and English Books 1, 2, 3, & 4

English Reading Comprehension for the Spanish Speaker Books 1, 2 & 3 contains twenty lessons to help Spanish-speaking students improve their reading comprehension skills. Each lesson includes two vocabulary pages, a visualization page, a fluency page, two comprehension skill pages, and an answer key. These are excellent books to use after completing *English Reading and Spelling for the Spanish Speaker Books 1,2 & 3*. Price is $15.95, size is 8 1/2 x11 and 161 pages. Book 1 ISBN 1-878253-37-9, Book 2 ISBN 1-878253-43-3, Book 3 ISBN 1-878253-44-1.

English Reading and Spelling for the Spanish Speaker Books 1, 2, 3, 4, 5 & 6 contain twenty lessons to help Spanish-speaking students learn to read and spell English. The books use a systematic approach in teaching the English speech sounds and other phonological skills. They also present basic sight words that are not phonetic. The word lists are in Spanish and English and all directions are in Spanish with English translations. Each book is $14.95 and approximately 142 pages. Book size is 8 1/2 x 11. Book 1 ISBN 1-878253-24-7, Book 2 ISBN 1-878253-25-5, Book 3 ISBN 1-878253-26-3, Book 4 ISBN 1-878253-29-8, Book 5 ISBN 1-878253-30-1, Book 6 ISBN 1-878253-35-2.

ENGLISH for the SPANISH SPEAKER Books 1, 2, 3, & 4 are English as a Second Language workbooks for ages 10 - adult. Each book is divided into eight lessons and is written in Spanish and English. Each lesson includes: vocabulary, a conversation, a story, four activity pages, an answer key, two dictionaries: English-Spanish and Spanish-English, a puzzle section, and an index. Each book is $12.95 and approximately 110 pages. Book size is 8 1/2 x 11. Book 1 ISBN 1-878253-07-7, Book 2 ISBN 1-878253-16-6, Book 3 ISBN 1-878253-17-4, Book 4 ISBN 1-878253-18-2; Book 1 Cassette ISBN 1-878253-21-2, Book 2 Cassette ISBN 1-878253-32-8, Book 3 Cassette ISBN 1-878253-33-6, Book 4 Cassette ISBN 1-878253-34-4.

SPANISH made FUN and EASY Books 1 & 2 are workbooks for ages 10 - adult. Each book includes stories, games, conversations, activity pages, vocabulary lists, dictionaries, and an index. The books are for beginning Spanish students; people who want to brush up on high school Spanish; or for Spanish speakers who want to learn how to read and write Spanish. Each book is $14.95 and 134 pages. Book size is 8 1/2 x 11. Book 1 ISBN 1-878253-42-5, Book 2 ISBN 1-878253-46-8.

HEALTH Easy to Read contains 21 easy to read stories. After each story is a vocabulary page, a grammar page, and a question and answer page. The stories are about changing people's life styles to reduce their risk of poor health and premature death. Book is $13.95 and has 118 pages. Book size is 8 1/2 x 11. ISBN 1-878253-41-7. Revised 2005.

United STATES of America Stories, Maps, Activities in SPANISH and ENGLISH Books 1, 2, 3, & 4 are easy to read books about the United States of America for ages 10 - adult. Each state is presented by a story, map, and activities. Each book contains information for 12 to 13 states and has an answer key and index. The states are presented in alphabetical order. Book size is 8 1/2 x 11. Each book is $14.95 and approximately 140 pages.
Book 1 ISBN 1-878253-23-9 Alabama through Idaho
Book 2 ISBN 1-878253-11-5 Illinois through Missouri
Book 3 ISBN 1-878253-12-3 Montana through Pennsylvania
Book 4 ISBN 1-878253-13-1 Rhode Island through Wyoming

Toll Free Ordering
1-800-214-8110
Monday-Friday 8am-5pm
Central Standard Time

Order On-Line
www.Fisher-Hill.com

Order by Fax
714-377-9495

Questions or Concerns
1-800-494-4652
714-377-9353

Fisher Hill

5267 Warner Ave., #166
Huntington Beach, CA 92649-4079
www.Fisher-Hill.com

Purchase Order Number: _____

Bill To:
Name: _____
Address: _____
City: _____ State _____ ZIP _____
Phone: _____

Ship To: (if different than billing address)
Name: _____
Address: _____
City: _____ State _____ ZiP _____
Phone: _____

QUANTITY	ISBN 1-878253-	BOOK TITLE	PRICE	AMOUNT
	37-9	English Reading Comprehension for the Spanish Speaker Book 1	$15.95	
	43-3	English Reading Comprehension for the Spanish Speaker Book 2	$15.95	
	44-1	English Reading Comprehension for the Spanish Speaker Book 3	$15.95	
	27-1	English Reading and Spelling for the Spanish Speaker Book 1	$14.95	
	25-5	English Reading and Spelling for the Spanish Speaker Book 2	$14.95	
	26-3	English Reading and Spelling for the Spanish Speaker Book 3	$14.95	
	29-8	English Reading and Spelling for the Spanish Speaker Book 4	$14.95	
	30-1	English Reading and Spelling for the Spanish Speaker Book 5	$14.95	
	35-2	English Reading and Spelling for the Spanish Speaker Book 6	$14.95	
	07-7	English For The Spanish Speaker Book 1	$12.95	
	21-2	English For The Spanish Speaker Book 1 Cassette	$10.95	
	20-4	English For The Spanish Speaker Book 1 and Cassette	$21.95	
	16-6	English For The Spanish Speaker Book 2	$12.95	
	32-8	English For The Spanish Speaker Book 2 Cassette	$10.95	
	38-7	English For The Spanish Speaker Book 2 and Cassette	$21.95	
	17-4	English For The Spanish Speaker Book 3	$12.95	
	33-6	English For The Spanish Speaker Book 3 Cassette	$10.95	
	39-5	English For The Spanish Speaker Book 3 and Cassette	$21.95	
	18-2	English For The Spanish Speaker Book 4	$12.95	
	34-4	English For The Spanish Speaker Book 4 Cassette	$10.95	
	40-9	English For The Spanish Speaker Book 4 and Cassette	$21.95	
	41-7	HEALTH Easy to Read	$13.95	
	23-9	USA Stories, Maps, Activities in Spanish & English Book 1	$14.95	
	11-5	USA Stories, Maps, Activities in Spanish & English Book 2	$14.95	
	12-3	USA Stories, Maps, Activities in Spanish & English Book 3	$14.95	
	13-1	USA Stories, Maps, Activities in Spanish & English Book 4	$14.95	
	42-5	SPANISH made FUN & EASY Book 1	$14.95	
	46-8	SPANISH made FUN & EASY Book 2	$14.95	
	MW920-2	Diccionario Español-Inglés	$6.50	
	MW852-4	Diccionario de Sinónimos y Antónimos en Inglés	$6.50	
	MW890-7	Juego de Diccionarios	$19.50	
	MW605-X	Dictionary of Basic English	$9.95	

Credit Card Information
Card Number: _____
Expiration Date: _____
Name: _____
Address: _____
City: _____ State _____ ZIP _____
Phone: _____

TOTAL _____

Add 7.75% for shipments to California addresses. SALES TAX _____

Add 10% of TOTAL for shipping. (Minimum $4.00) SHIPPING _____

PAYMENT _____

BALANCE DUE _____